PANTHER TANK

Panzerkampfwagen V Panther (SdKfz 171)

First published in May 2019
Reprinted September 2020 and July 2022

A catalogue record for this book is available from the British Library.

ISBN 978 1 78521 214 7

Library of Congress control no. 2018938915

Published by J H Haynes & Co. Ltd.,
Sparkford, Yeovil, Somerset BA22 7JJ, UK.
Tel: 01963 440635
Int. tel: +44 1963 440635
Website: www.haynes.com

Haynes North America Inc.,
859 Lawrence Drive, Newbury Park,
California 91320, USA.

Printed in India.

Senior Commissioning Editor: Jonathan Falconer
Copy editor: Michelle Tilling
Proof reader: Penny Housden
Indexer: Peter Nicholson
Page design: James Robertson

Acknowledgements

All pictures are from the Thomas Anderson Collection. I owe a debt of thanks to Thomas for his generosity in allowing me to use so many of his photographs. The only section in the book where he is formally credited thus (TA) is in Chapter 4 where it is necessary to distinguish those he has supplied of the Panthers at the Munster Museum and at Koblenz from the bulk of photographs in that section which are of the Panther Ausf G at the Tank Museum, Bovington, in the UK, and which were taken specially for this book by their official photographer. Those few images from my own collection are credited thus (Author). Those that are credited as (NARA) are from the US National Archives.

I wish also to thank the staff in the archive section at the Tank Museum for all their help in the provision of documentation on the Panther.

PANTHER TANK

Panzerkampfwagen V Panther (SdKfz 171)

Enthusiasts' Manual

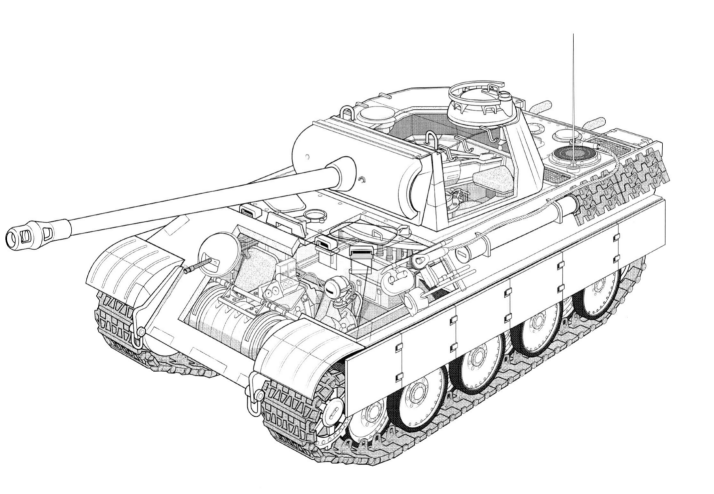

An insight into the design, construction and operation of the finest medium tank of the Second World War

Mark Healy

Contents

OPPOSITE A Waffen-SS Panther navigates its way past the Arc de Triomphe in Paris, June 1944. *(Bundesarchiv Bild 101I-721-0395-22)*

RIGHT A Panther D prior to the beginning of its debut combat operation during Operation Citadel in July 1943.

Chapter One

The Panther story

From conception to production

It was from the German Army's bruising encounters with the new generation of superior Soviet armour of the KV series and in particular the T-34 medium tank that the specification for a new and superior German panzer arose. The resultant Panther medium tank is still regarded by many to this day to have been the best of the conflict.

OPPOSITE The first Panther fitted with a weight to simulate the turret was retained by MAN and put through its paces at the company's test track. The second, seen here, was fitted with a turret, albeit not one that would enter production, and was despatched to the Army Proving Ground at Kummersdorf for trials.

ABOVE Panzer IIIs represented the cutting edge of the *Panzertruppe* in the invasion of Russia on 22 June 1941.

It was during the course of 15 May 1942 that the managing director of Maschinenfabrik Augsburg–Nürnberg company (hereafter MAN) received an important, albeit not unexpected, phone call from Oberst Fichtner, the Head of the Panzer und Motorisierungsabtielung (Panzer and Motorised Equipment Branch – hereafter Wa Prüf 6) of the Heereswaffenamt (German Army Weapons Agency) in Berlin. What Fichtner relayed was good news for the company, stating that following the decision of the Führer to endorse the final recommendation of the Tank Commission that had been set up specifically for the purpose of evaluating the two designs competing for the production of a new medium tank for the German Army, he had accepted that the MAN proposal should be adopted over that of the competing Daimler-Benz design. With this award came the order for MAN to begin the process of preparing for series production. In addition, the company was ordered to incorporate a number of technical modifications to its design, one of which had been stipulated by Hitler himself – that of increasing the thickness of the glacis plate on the front of the new tank by 20mm from its originally specified 60mm to 80mm. The

weight of the new panzer had thus increased significantly, having grown over the period of its design gestation from 32.5 tons of the original specification to its final combat weight of some 44 tons.

When first committed to combat in July 1943, the Panther, as this new design had been named, was by far and away the heaviest medium tank to be fielded by any of the major combatants in the Second World War. It was twice as heavy as the Panzer III – the machine it had been designed to replace. This begs the question as to why it was that such a heavy fighting vehicle would assume this role when its predecessor had weighed in at a mere 22.3 tons in its final production iteration as a medium tank. This itself was some 7 tons heavier than the first model of this type, which had weighed in at just 15.4 tons when produced in 1936. Certainly before 22 June 1941 – the date on which Nazi Germany invaded the Soviet Union – the notion of a medium tank of the weight and size of the new Panther would have been viewed with scepticism by German tank designers. Indeed, ongoing work on the then envisaged replacement for the Mark III saw it also as being in the 20-ton range, this being viewed at the time as the optimum weight for a tank of this class.

What had prompted a change in the assumptions regarding future design parameters for a replacement medium tank for the German Army had been its encounter with a totally new and unknown generation of Soviet medium and heavy tanks following the launch of the Russian Campaign. The result was to render all existing German tank designs, and even those still on the drawing boards and under development, as technically obsolescent. Of these, it was the T-34 medium tank that was to provide the greatest shock to German complacency and provide the impetus that was to lead in due course to the Panther. According to Dr Wiebecke, the Chief Engineer on the design of the Panther, when interviewed by Major R.E. Kaufman of the US Ordnance Corps in August 1945, it was explicitly understood by himself and all others involved in the design and production of this new medium tank that 'the Panther had been designed to cope with the Russian T-34'. But as we shall see, it was expected that it would do more than just secure parity with the Russian design. It was required to be superior to any existing and near-future enemy tank design – whether from the East or West – such that it would, once available, assure battlefield dominance for the *Schnelltruppen* (fast troops or rapid forces) – the term employed to designate the panzer and motorised infantry divisions.

Relating the Panther story thus requires us to return to the period before June 1941 to explore in outline – for here is not the place to dwell in detail on German planning for Operation Barbarossa – and touch on the assumptions that underpinned the invasion of the Soviet Union. For it was the totally false nature of many of these assumptions that was to lead, in due course, to the creation of the Panther (and in much wider terms to the defeat of Nazi Germany). On the eve of the launch of Operation Barbarossa on 22 June 1941, it was the overweening and common expectation of the political leadership of Nazi Germany and of the Wehrmacht High Command that the Soviet Union would be vanquished in a military campaign lasting between just nine and twelve weeks.

Dealing with Russia – a lesser affair than France!

Following the invasion of the West on 10 May 1940 and the subsequent conquest and surrender of France and the Low Countries by the end of June, it was the shared opinion of Hitler and the senior German military that in defeating France in a six-week campaign they had eliminated Germany's greatest military opponent and had thus fought their most difficult campaign. As such, the common perception was that any future conflict with the Soviet Union would prove to be a much lesser affair, with Hitler saying so barely days after the French surrender when he opined to General Keitel that 'a campaign against Russia would be a sand table exercise in comparison with the Western Campaign'. In this the German leader was hardly a lone voice as many of the senior *Feldherren* were of the view that 'that not only was a showdown with Bolshevism necessary and inevitable but also that Germany could defeat Russia easily'.

Hitler's Barbarossa Directive of December 1940 drew heavily on the two working plans for the campaign prepared earlier by General Marcks of the 9th Army and Colonel Lossberg of the Oberkommando des Heers (OKH). Although they differed in detail, both were unequivocal that:

> at no point in the planning process did Lossberg reveal any doubts about the feasibility of that goal: like Marcks he assumed that the Russians possessed neither the operational skill to conduct a fighting withdrawal nor the reserves they would need to halt the invasion in the interior of the country.

This profoundly derogatory view of Germany's *supposed* Eastern ally stemmed from a view of Russia whose provenance went back many years. This had been inherited and then deepened by the Nazis' racist theories. Russia was still regarded as a 'colossus with feet of clay', hence Hitler's grandiloquent claim '. . . we have only to kick in the front door and the whole rotten structure will come tumbling down'. Thus all German planning was predicated on this primary assumption, with the corollary being that the Red Army, notwithstanding its great size, was simply not up to the task of opposing an invasion by the Wehrmacht, now operating at the very height of its power and effectiveness.

The key factor in common within the planning documents for the invasion of the Soviet Union produced by officers of the Army appointed to prepare them was the central role allotted to the *Schnelltruppen*. Indeed, there was no ambiguity in either plan prepared by Marcks and Lossberg that it was these forces that were seen as being the key to securing the rapid defeat of the Red Army and the realisation of victory over the Soviet Union in the short time allotted to the military operation. Nor was it believed that the Red Army's tank force could provide any meaningful opposition to the *Panzertruppe* once the Eastern Campaign began.

It was therefore paradoxical that the conviction within the German Army that their armoured forces were so superior to those of the Red Army was itself grounded, as indeed was so much else that was believed about the Soviet state, on limited and flawed intelligence. Small wonder then that in the absence of such, the view of the Red Army prevalent in the German High Command and of its tank arm was inferred from the past:

> *Russian performance in Spain, Poland and Finland . . . and what they saw did not impress them. The operations revealed a number of serious problems in the Soviet army, although the Germans also noted Russian efforts at remediation, they did not expect to see significant improvement for years.*

Indeed, as late as May 1941, having witnessed the military parade in Red Square, Colonel Krebs, the new German military attaché in Moscow, had reported back to Berlin that from his observations 'it would take the Red Army Officer class twenty years to reach Wehrmacht levels of professionalism'.

His words at the time merely served to reinforce the German conviction in 1941 that '. . . behind this Russian ineffectiveness . . . lay the purges that Stalin had carried out in his officer corps in 1937 and 1938'.

And of the many thousands of officers, from the highest to the lowest, who died with a bullet to the back of the head or who disappeared into the camps of the Gulag, a disproportionate number came from the armoured force. This was to profoundly impact on the effectiveness of the Red Army tank force, which between then and June 1941, fell victim to changing doctrinal fashions which prefigured massive organisational changes. These flip-flopped from seeing tanks first returned to an infantry-support role in 1939, and then once again, just over a year later, following the German victory over France, to a complete volte-face with the order issued to reintegrate tanks into new, large Mechanised Corps, of which there were 29 on strength on 22 June 1941. Of these new formations, most were still many months away from a proper reorganisation, which included a massive retraining programme and the induction of new, modern equipment. Indeed, the planning for such was predicated on the assumption that this massive programme would not be completed before 1942 at the earliest, by which time it was estimated that the Red Army would have received upwards of 20,000 new tanks. The Red Army – and not just the armoured forces – was thus caught at its weakest and most inept, indeed at the very nadir of its effectiveness, by the timing of the German invasion.

Flawed German assumptions about the Red Army's tank force

The German High Command recognised that while:

> *the Red Army's armour was regarded as an elite force, it was believed that, because of inadequate combat training and training in co-operation with other branches, it was incapable of conducting a modern war of movement with far-ranging operations by compact formations.*

This of course was, by the summer of 1941, the demonstrated forte of the German Army and the basis of their untrammelled optimism as to the likely outcome of the Russian Campaign.

Nor was it believed that the tanks in service with the Red Army could match those of the *Panzertruppe*. While acknowledging that the Red Army's tank park was large, and that it would certainly outnumber those deployed by the Germans for Barbarossa, there was no certainty as to what that figure actually was. Nonetheless, that uncertainty did not embrace the quantity postulated by General Heinz Guderian, regarded by many as 'the father of the panzer arm'. Guderian, having turned to the written word in 1937 to advocate his case for the primacy of the tank and mobile warfare for the new Wehrmacht in his book *Achtung Panzer!*, had given a figure for the Red Army as already possessing a tank park of 10,000 machines. He was vehemently derided and this number ridiculed as nonsense by many within the German Army at the time. But within weeks of the invasion of Russia in June 1941, the vast quantity of Soviet armour that had been destroyed in combat or abandoned by the Red Army pointed all too clearly to this 1937 figure being a profound underestimation. The true figure for Red Army tank strength was 22,600

as of 22 June 1941 (though Stalin, in December 1941, put this figure even higher, at 24,000). Be that as it may, the bulk of this huge number – some 20,500 machines – had been eliminated by December 1941. However, this catastrophic loss was as much explicable in terms of the dire condition of the Soviet tank arm and of the ineptness of its operation as it was a product of German armoured prowess.

But one matter in particular – that is in the total failure of German intelligence to detect the existence of a new generation of technically superior heavy and medium tanks that were being delivered to the Red Army from early 1940 and which were available in some numbers by the time of the invasion – was to have profound consequences for the *Panzertruppe.* It was ignorance of the existence of these new machines that also goes some way to account for Germany's confidence that it could easily dispose of the Red Army tank force, for it was presumed that the types that were being operated by the Red Army were all known quantities and were adjudged as being technically inferior to those operated

ABOVE At the time of Operation Barbarossa, the Panzer IV was regarded by the Germans as a heavy tank and was still serving in the support role to the more numerous Panzer III.

by the *Panzertruppe*. This was especially so with respect to the key types operated by the latter, these being the Panzer III (medium) and the Panzer IV (heavy) support tank. Of the total number of 3,266 panzers (including command tanks but excluding self-propelled guns) committed in the 17 tank divisions employed in the invasion, the most powerfully armed German machine was the latter, with the 75mm L/24 low-velocity main weapon. Some 444 of these were committed to the invasion. The Mark III constituted the primary tank of the *Panzertruppe* with 966 of the total, with 707 of these armed with the improved 50mm L/42 gun and the remaining 259 still equipped with the original 37mm weapon that had proven so inadequate in the French Campaign. Nonetheless, Russian armour was held in such

low regard that the Chief of the General Staff, Colonel General Halder, was to crow in his diary days before Barbarossa began that the 50mm-armed Panzer III would devastate enemy tanks once the invasion commenced.

Even though the bulk of the remaining German armour was in the form of light tanks with the Panzer 35(t) and 38(t) also employing a 37mm main gun and the Panzer II with the 20mm cannon as its main weapon, these were still deemed more than adequate to deal with a Russian tank park made up of machines familiar to the Germans since the Spanish Civil War. Other types that were known quantities had become familiar through having been seen in military displays in Red Square and witnessed by Germans 'in action' when the Red Army had moved into western Poland in late September 1939 and also during the Winter War with Finland in 1939–40. Guderian had rather disparagingly written of the T-26 and BT series tanks he saw in Poland 'as obsolete machines based upon older Western designs'. Nonetheless, it was the cumulation of this massively flawed underestimate of the actual and latent might of the USSR and of the potential of the Red Army's tank force that so coloured German perceptions of the enemy they were about to encounter. And it would be within the first few days of the invasion that the *Panzertruppe* would find itself having to deal with new Soviet machines that totally undermined many of the complacent assumptions that governed their assessment of the Red Army, and which would, in due course, lead to the specification for a new medium tank to replace the Panzer Mark III.

The KV-1 and T-34 shock

Unbeknown to the Germans, at least 1,000 T-34s were in service at the time of the invasion, the tank having entered service in 1940. Seen here is a T-34/1940 model.

Although the encounter with the KV-1 and -2 heavy tanks and the T-34 medium tank came as a bolt from the blue for the German units that found themselves having to contend with these types, it is not the case that the Germans had no intimation of their existence whatsoever, but possessed nothing more than that.

Even as Barbarossa was being prepared for in the spring of 1941, the German tank industry was playing host to a visiting delegation of Soviet officials who had come to view its latest products. This might seem strange given that the invasion was planned for June, but Hitler, in ordering that they be shown everything, was perhaps hoping that the experience would serve to send them home somewhat intimidated. If so, then this was not at all the reaction that it engendered. Shown the latest models of the Panzers III and IV, the visitors complained that the Germans were holding out on them – surely these did not represent the latest and heaviest of the panzers that they were building? Even though reassured that they were being shown everything, the Russians still expressed their doubts with their continuing incredulity prompting their hosts to infer that such a reaction would only make sense if it was the Russians who were already developing and even producing new medium and heavy tanks of which the Germans had no knowledge.

The response of the Germans to their suspicions and then to the knowledge (if they had gained such) that the KV-1/2 heavy tanks and the T-34 medium had been in production since the previous year would have profoundly unnerved them. Indeed, by 22 June 1941, the total number of these machines in service with the Red Army already amounted to some 500 of the former and 1,000 of the latter – a figure corresponding to nearly half of the total number of tanks the Germans committed to the invasion. Here is not the place to go into the history of the development of either tank, but, for further information, see this author's previous title for Haynes, which covers that of the T-34.

It was the KV heavy tank that first saw service in trials at the tail-end of the Russo-Finnish Winter War of 1939/40, with production

examples leaving the Kirov factory in Leningrad and entering service in 1940. The T-34 medium tank had also been slated for testing in the Winter War, but this was concluded before the prototypes were ready. The T-34 shared the same engine and 7.62cm (76mm) main armament as the heavy tank and the first production model – the T-34/76A – left the main production line at the Komintern Plant No 183 in Kharkov in the first half of 1940, and, in 1941, a much smaller number from the STZ site in Stalingrad. In less troubled times, the Soviet state would have taken every opportunity to publicise their new medium and heavy tanks for propagandistic reasons, but neither the May Day nor the October parades in Red Square of 1940 nor the May Day parade in 1941 at the same venue, saw either of these new machines on display. Despite Stalin's almost obsessional insistence that Hitler would never attempt to attack Russia while Britain remained undefeated, he nevertheless ordered that neither of these new machines be displayed. Only those tank types that the Germans were already familiar with and had demeaned as being obsolescent were to be seen – reinforcing no doubt their conviction that there was nothing to be concerned about.

With respect to its design, while the T-34's thick, sloping armour was to prove highly effective, the two-man turret did not permit an easy service of the main gun, nor of its targeting, as the tank commander had to double up his roles by also functioning as the gun-aimer. He was hamstrung in either – executing one task or the other – he could not do both. Nor did he possess a cupola permitting him the superior situational awareness of the battlefield that was standard for the commanders of the German Mark III and IV. Once shut down, his optics were also somewhat poor and limited in number. The majority of T-34 tank crews were poorly trained; indeed, many went into combat with just a few hours of operating experience under their belts. And most of these new machines were encountered not in mass, but in driblets – the very opposite of what Guderian had demanded as to how the panzers should be properly employed. Indeed, the use of these new machines in 1941 still echoed the by now discarded infantry support tactics used by the Red Army between 1939 and 1940. Radios were also in very short supply, so command and control was exceedingly poor, with much reliance placed, as in the older designs, on the employment of signal flags. They thus lacked what was perhaps one of the principal means that permitted the Germans to outfight the Russians – their superior command and control – notwithstanding their far fewer numbers, and relative to the T-34 and KV-1 and -2, their inferior technology.

It was the 1st and 6th Panzer Divisions that had one of the first encounters with these new Russian tanks and although T-34s were among those that attacked the German formation, it was the super heavy KV-1 and KV-2s that made the greatest impression. Belonging to the Soviet 5th Tank Division of the 3rd Mechanised Corps, the Germans found themselves bound up in an ongoing three-day tank battle near the town of Raseinai. The arrival of General Reinhardt, the commander of XXXXI Panzer Corps, at the divisional HQ, brought the news that 'the Russian anti-tank gun 37mm is as useless against our new tank armour plating as our 50mm/L42 gun [in the Mark III – author] and 50mm anti-tank gun was against the armour of medium Russian tanks'. It was further pointed out in a reference to what must be assumed to be the 7.62cm weapon that 'the Soviet heavy anti-tank gun is a frightful weapon'. This of course was the same calibre gun as that mounted on the T-34 and KVs.

A measure of the near-panic induced by these 'unknown' Soviet types can be gleaned from a message received at the HQ of 1st Panzer Division in the early hours of 25 June 1941, wherein it detailed that the 2nd Battalion of the Armoured Rifle Regiment 1 had been overrun, conveying more than just a hint of panic:

Neither the infantry's anti-tank guns, nor those of our own PanzerJäger platoons (six anti-tank guns of 50mm), nor the tank cannon of the medium and heavy German tanks are able to pierce the plating of the heavy Russian tanks! What can be done to stop those heavy Russian tanks?

What was done was to improvise – employing the by now proven 88mm flak gun as an anti-tank weapon: neither the T-34 nor the KVs could withstand its firepower. In addition, medium and heavy artillery pieces fired over open sights and on a flat trajectory with infantry braving the proximity of these beasts to lay satchel charges on them. The panzers, too, responded quickly – firing at point-blank range with special ammunition at what became recognised as the vulnerable points on the Russian tanks, such as the turret rings or the rear plates of the hulls where the armour was thinner. From the outset, the forces of Army Group South, particularly those deployed in the northern sector, had to contend with much larger numbers of these new Soviet machines. Many of both types were encountered in what some have called the biggest tank battle of the war at the Brody–Lutsk–Rovno axis.

In accounts of these events it can be very glib to relate them, then jump ahead to consider the steps taken to redress the apparent superiority of the T-34 and KV series. In actuality, this misses what was clearly a profoundly difficult moment for the German Army. Within two days of the invasion, many of the comfortable assumptions about the nature of the Red Army and its level of technology had been shown to be wrong. It also served notice that 'ten years of anti-tank training and weapons development by the German side vanished into thin air when 37mm and 50mm projectiles ineffectively bounced off of T-34 and KV hulls'. It was a proverbial 'shaking of the foundations'.

Oberst H. Ritgen, who was serving as an adjutant in a battalion of Panzer Regiment 11 of the 6th Panzer Division at the time of the Battle

at Raseinai, offered up the following telling reflection on what the encounter with these new Russian machines implied:

> German tanks had hitherto been intended mainly to fight enemy infantry and their supporting arms. *From now on* the main threat was the enemy tank itself, and the need to 'kill' it at as great a range as possible led to the design of longer-barrelled guns of larger calibre [author's emphasis]. *Tank guns of less than 75mm became more or less useless; and until HEAT (High Explosive Anti-Tank) ammunition was supplied in 1942, the L/24 75mm gun of the PzKpfw IV, with its low velocity of 385m/sec, was generally ineffective against the new Russian vehicles.*

Such a perceptive analysis prefigured the specification for the Panther and the priority of firepower in all new German tank designs. It was therefore fortuitous that barely weeks after the beginning of Barbarossa the decision to order a new tank gun that could do what

Ritgen required, had been placed. Although intended originally for the VK 45.01 – the design that would become the Tiger I heavy tank – it was purely coincidental that Wa Prüf 6 had placed a contract with Rheinmetall (hereafter RM) of Düsseldorf in mid-July 1941 for just such a weapon, months before the concept of the new Panther medium tank was even a glimmer in any German tank designer's mind's eye! While Fichtner had not specified the calibre of the weapon to RM, it was required that whatever they determined upon be able to penetrate 140mm of armour at 1,000m range. While initially they created a gun of 60mm of L/60 calibre, this was subsequently increased to an L/70 calibre and by February 1942 the company had also designed the turret to house this weapon. Although passed over for the Tiger tank, it would be adopted by MAN for its new medium tank proposal.

Further evidence of the profound fright generated by the T-34 and KVs can be gleaned from an observation by Edel Ligenthal (later Brigadier General), who at the time was a company commander in 11th Panzer Division that found itself engaging T-34s as early as 23 June. He noted how the enemy tanks knocked out German tanks relatively easily but that the 50mm and low-velocity 75mm shells proved ineffective against the T-34, even in flank fire as close as 300m. Following the Soviet withdrawal, he took the opportunity to examine a number of machines that had been abandoned by the Soviets. Commenting that they had not received any information about the tank type, he noted that its armour plating, munitions and mobility were superior to those of any German tank. His real concern and that of others who also encountered these new Soviet 'monster tanks' was the impact on the morale of German troops: 'This was a shocking recognition to the German tank and tank destroyer [PanzerJäger] and our knees were weak for a time.'

At the behest of the OKH and Dr Todt, the Head of the Ministry for Weapons and Ammunition, Oberst Fichtner was instructed to inform the relevant companies then engaged in developing new tanks in the VK 20 class to cease work on their designs as the decision had been taken, in the light of the encounter with and impact of the T-34, to develop a new and heavier medium tank in the 30-ton class. This decision did not go down well as it was felt among the Wa Prüf 6 that their opinions had been overridden and that all the work that had been carried out on this weight class thus far (it still being the case that Wa Prüf 6 believed that a medium tank of about 20 tons represented the optimum weight for a tank of this class) would now be wasted and that it would take valuable time to develop a new tank. Nor was it believed that it would be possible to produce a tank in the 30-ton class in the numbers required. But the simple fact was that a 20-ton design could not mount a weapon powerful enough to defeat these new Soviet designs, and they were thus obsolescent.

It would seem that even as Oberst Fichtner prepared to lead a tank commission to Russia, the fate of the Panzer Mark III, as the primary medium tank of the Panzertruppe, had also been sealed with Hitler himself some weeks earlier – he having described the Mark III as a 'failed design'. It was hardly that, having satisfied the design criteria for a German medium tank as issued in the mid-1930s and had proven to be very effective in all the campaigns in which it had served – until, of course, Russia. The decision to embrace a heavier replacement – the machine that would in due course lead to the Panther – also brought down the curtain on the earlier July decision to produce a further 7,992 of this type to equip the proposed expansion of the Panzerwaffe to 36 divisions, with this unrealisable idea being allowed to die a death. And even though the Panzer III would continue to be built and upgraded – the final variant built as a medium tank being the Panzer III Ausf M, leaving the production line in October 1942 with the last of this variant not being completed until February 1943 – the decision to terminate its production had already in principle been made. Quite simply, its inability to mount a weapon more powerful than the 50mm L/60 introduced on the Ausf J condemned the design as a medium tank. Its place in the inventory of the German Army was now to be filled by an as yet undesigned, heavier and more powerfully armed tank. It was in quest of the information needed to help frame the specification for such a tank that Fichtner and others were now to head eastward to Russia.

The Panzer Commission to Russia

The arrival on 18 November 1941 of a commission of the great and the good of the German tank industry in Russia at the headquarters of Guderian's 2nd *Panzergruppe* had been prompted by the clamour, not just from the *Panzertruppe* but also from representatives of the infantry, who were demanding better equipment to combat the T-34 and KVs. That this powerful and influential commission was briefed on the tank situation by Guderian is testimony to the very high regard in which his expertise and status in all matters pertaining to armoured warfare was held. It would seem, however, that up until the encounter of 4th Panzer Division with a larger number of T-34s and KVs at Mtsensk on 7 October, he does not appear to have taken too much notice of these new Russian machines.

In his extensive report on the encounter, Freiherr von Langermann, the commander of the 4th Panzer Division, noted that at Mtsensk the Soviets 'deployed their tanks en masse for the first time' – something which the Germans had been spared thus far by virtue of the Russians employing them in ones and twos. In consequence of the Russians adopting these new tactics, the Germans found themselves fighting some 'very hard tank battles', and came off the worse with panzer losses being high. German losses are still a matter of dispute with the higher figure claiming that 133 tanks were lost, along with 49 artillery pieces and infantry equivalent to regimental strength. This was a severe bloody nose and is explicable primarily due to the Russians standing off and not closing with the German armour, employing the greater range of their main armament to assail the German tanks, firing at them from 1,000m range and knocking out many panzers, some of which were:

> . . . split open or the complete commanders' cupola of the PzKpfw III and IV flew off from one hit. . . . In addition to the superior weapons effectiveness and stronger armour, the 26-ton [T-34] is faster, more manoeuvrable and the turret traverse mechanism clearly superior.

Langermann continued by lauding other aspects of its design, also noting that it was bound to be encountered in much larger numbers in the future. The upshot of all of this was that Guderian employed this very detailed report as the basis of his own presentation which he delivered to the members of the Tank Commission on 18 November even as Operation Typhoon – the offensive to capture Moscow – was still ongoing.

Led by the aforementioned Oberst Fichtner and colleagues Oberbaurat Kniepkamp and Major Ruden from Wa Prüf 6, the representatives of the German tank industry included Professor Dr F. Porsche, Direktor Dr Rohland of the Vereinigte Stahlwerke (Chairman of the Main Committee for Tanks in the Ministry for Ammunition and Weapons), Direktor Wunderlich of Daimler-Benz, Direktor Dr Hacker of Steyr in Austria, Direktor Dorn of Krupp-Kanonen, Obering Aders of Henschel, Obering Zimmer of RM and, last but not least, Ing Oswal of MAN. These men comprised the leading lights of all the major companies involved in tank production in the Reich, such

LEFT General Heinz Guderian, regarded as the father of the *Panzertruppe*, hosted the commission of senior executives from Germany's tank industry when they visited Russia on 18 November 1941. He argued for the creation and production of a new tank to defeat the T-34 and KV tanks.

was the importance attached to this visit to the Eastern Front, for it was out of this consultation that there was to emerge, in fairly rapid order, the specification for what would in due course become the Panther. Before their departure, Guderian delivered one final address in which he distilled his observations by stating that for all new tank designs it would be necessary to ensure that the priority became firstly the provision of heavier armament, followed by higher tactical mobility and thence better armour protection.

On their return to Germany, Fichtner and his colleagues in Wa Prüf 6 moved rapidly to consolidate the recommendations and create a specification for issue to industry. On 25 November, just four days after the return from Russia, Wa Prüf 6 issued this to just two companies – Daimler-Benz (hereafter DB) and MAN – for the creation of a new tank in the 30-ton class under the designation VK 30.02. The basic specification, as laid out below, was further agreed in another meeting on 9 December:

VK 30.02
Combat weight: 32.5 tons
Power-to-weight ratio: 16hp/ton
Ground pressure (bar): 0.88
Armament: 75mm L/70
Armour front/side/rear (mm): 60*/40/40
Fuel capacity: 720 litres (petrol)
Range: 240km
Maximum hull width: 3,150mm
Maximum height: 2,990mm
Engine size: 650–700 metric hp
* Later raised to 80mm.

The manner in which the two companies interpreted this specification was to lead to two very different designs. Indeed, in the case of the MAN company, the specification was delivered in person by Oberbaurat Kniepkamp who had a particular interest in seeing that the MAN design won. Not only had he begun his career with the company in the early 1920s, but he had been instrumental in the late 1930s in helping to bring about the development work on torsion bar suspension systems and the idea of interleaved running gears, which was to be employed in the submission from that company.

In the meantime, the *Kraftfahrversuchsstelle* or motor test facility at the Army Proving Ground at Kummersdorf had received a T-34 in early December which was examined as a matter of urgency. The resulting report concluded with Oberst Dipl.Ing Esser, the commander of the facility, praising the Russian tank, his parting observation being that it should simply be 'copied' and issued to the *Panzertruppe.* That was, however, never going to happen, even if it was the case that many of the desirable features of the T-34 would find their way into the new medium tank design.

By early December, the war situation for Germany had been fundamentally transformed. Even before Operation Typhoon had stalled short of Moscow and the Red Army had gone over to a completely unexpected counter-offensive on 5 December, it had become apparent that Barbarossa had failed. Then Hitler, just five days after the Japanese attack on Pearl Harbor, declared war on the USA. The whole strategic situation was thus radically changed and in a manner totally inimical to Nazi Germany's longer-term military fortunes. Consciousness of the reality of a much wider war impacted on the selection process that now prevailed between the two designs. The underlying imperative in the whole process was one in which this new machine had to be placed in production, and thence in combat, as soon as possible. This necessarily had consequences, in that the rapid gestation time for this new and complex machine and the necessary short cuts taken in the provision of equipment to enable it to happen generated problems and weaknesses in the construction and thence operation of the Panther that would not be resolved before the war's end in May 1945. Nonetheless, the fact that Germany was now fighting a much wider war fed into the VK 30.02 in that as it was understood by both DB and MAN that they were designing a tank that would need to be able to counter and be superior to all foreign designs that the German Army would expect to face for the foreseeable future. Ensuring that the new Panther, as the design had been designated, would achieve dominance over the T-34 was also presumed to be the manner in which those wider concerns would also be realised.

There can be only one

A meeting was held in Berlin on 22 January 1942 at the Heereswaffenamt to discuss the VK 30.02 proposals, it being acknowledged from the outset that with time of the essence only one design would be selected and placed in production. The leading lights of Wa Prüf 6 were in attendance, as were representatives of MAN and Daimler-Benz. Dr Wiebecke, of the former, was to relate that:

> the combat weight of 32.5 tons, decided upon in the meeting of the 9 December has increased to about 36 metric tons through modification of the design during different meetings. Wa Prüf 6 had created a model based on this new data [this was a conceptual model, not a competing design].

Whether or not the intention of DB was to steal a march on the opposition, they took the opportunity to present a model of their proposed design. Wiebecke was complimentary as to its appearance:

> Its appearance is very attractive. It has a rear drive, an open suspension and a pointed hull front as in the Russian T-34. At a meeting on 23 January both models are to be displayed in Hitler's headquarters [it is presumed that he means models of the DB and MAN designs]. Hitler's decision was to be quickly reported.

THE 'DB PANTHER'

Of the two competing designs for the contract to build the VK 30.02, the DB proposal drew more heavily on the design of the T-34. Both designs successfully (on paper, that is) addressed the tactical requirements as laid down by the Wa Prüf 6. Superficially, the two designs appeared similar in that they both incorporated the same sloping armour and the same armament in the form of the 75mm L/70 cannon, but thereafter matters diverged.

DB proposed the development of its own turret which was problematic for them in that it would take time to develop and the chassis could not take the already developed RM turret (the MAN design could). The turret ring was 50mm smaller on the DB design with the RM gun needing to be modified to fit into the turret. Other problems identified by the Tank Commission set up to evaluate the two designs was that it was felt that the turret optics were more vulnerable. Thus the DB turret was rejected and there was no alternative turret for the DB design. There was no opportunity to address this problem as time was of the essence. The new medium tank had to be put into production as soon as possible.

The DB design was praised as, like the T-34, it had the engine in the rear, which powered rear-mounted drive sprockets. It thus freed up more space for the crew.

However, the DB 'Panther' design held less fuel than its competitor – 550 litres compared to the MAN's 750. This had a significant impact on the range of the machine – a telling negative factor. The suspension of the DB differed to that of the MAN proposal in being of a leaf spring design, albeit with overlapping road wheels which also led to the track being 120mm narrower than that of the MAN Panther.

In spite of Hitler's support for the DB design, it was the contention of the Wa Prüf 6 in the form of Fichtner and Kniepkamp that the MAN torsion bar suspension was the favoured choice, a view reflected in the special Tank Commission's recommendation that the MAN design be awarded the contract for the new medium tank. After losing the contract DB was co-opted into the expanded MAN-designed Panther manufacturing programme.

BELOW No photographs survive of anything other than models to illustrate how DB's proposal for the new Panther tank would have appeared. What is clear is its great similarity to the T-34.

Indeed, the Führer too regarded the DB design as 'attractive' and favoured it over the MAN proposal, believing it 'to be superior to the MAN Panther'. In consequence of which, his new armaments minister, Albert Speer – the former incumbent of the office, Professor Todt, having been killed in an air crash early in February – recommended on 5 March that DB be given a contract for 200 of their design. This was not at all to the liking of either Fichtner or Kniepkamp, both of whom had expressed views that clearly favoured the MAN design. The upshot of this divergence of opinion was the establishment of a commission appointed by Hitler to make an objective assessment of the competing designs and recommend which would go forward for production.

Under the supervision and guidance of Oberst Thomale of the OKH Department Isp 6 and Professor Dr Ing von Eberhorst of the Technische Hochschule in Dresden, the commission first met at the beginning of May 1942. Having to hand a complete set of drawings and specifications for both designs, the assessment began – it being understood by all involved that their deliberations had to be governed by a number of overriding concerns:

- The first was the absolute priority given to the need to get the new machine into service no later than the summer of 1943. This could only be facilitated if production began at the end of 1942.
- Given the absolute need that the new machine be qualitatively superior to any machine fielded by the enemy, so as to negate their numerical superiority, the new panzer had to be produced to the highest standard. Such could not be realised, it was believed, by mass production.
- It was also understood, that if this new panzer were to be in service for the summer of 1943, the chosen design had to eschew any new technologies that would delay this.

Following a round of four intensive meetings in Berlin, it was on 11 May that the commission reported to the Chairman of the Tank Commission, Prof Dr Ing F. Porsche, that its members had unanimously agreed to recommend that the MAN design proposal be accepted. Two days later the findings were presented to Hitler who agreed to them a day later, prompting the call to MAN on 15 May, which is where we began this account.

What was it that the commission had accepted that made the MAN design the preferred option, notwithstanding Hitler's earlier enthusiasm for the losing DB design?

The essentials of the MAN Panther

The MAN Panther was essentially an extrapolation of their cancelled VK 20.02(M) design, keeping many of its key features. The hull retained the same angles for its sloping hull armour, this having been adopted for the VK 20.02(M) in light of those employed by the T-34. This earlier design was also intended to be equipped with a torsion bar system but employed only six overlapping road wheels whereas MAN's VK 30.02 proposal would utilise eight to take account of the new machine's greater size and weight.

Fichtner and Kniepkamp's support for the MAN design and underwritten by the decision of the Tank Commission laid great stress on the efficacy of the torsion bar suspension system of their Panther design.

In contra-distinction to that employed on the DB design, that on the MAN Panther employed a double torsion bar spring which was believed to offer a better ride for the crew over rough terrain. It was thus deemed to provide a superior gun platform. This was essential as it was recognised as a point of principle that: 'the tank's sole mission was to destroy the enemy. This it did with its weapons, not with the chassis. As a result, the function of the chassis was to support the role of the weapon in destroying the enemy.'

- Furthermore, the employment of a torsion bar system permitted a slightly wider hull, which in turn allowed the MAN Panther to carry 200 litres more fuel than that of the DB design – 750 versus 550 – thereby conferring on it greater range on hard road surfaces and cross-country. The difference was significant in both cases – a matter of importance when in combat. In terms of

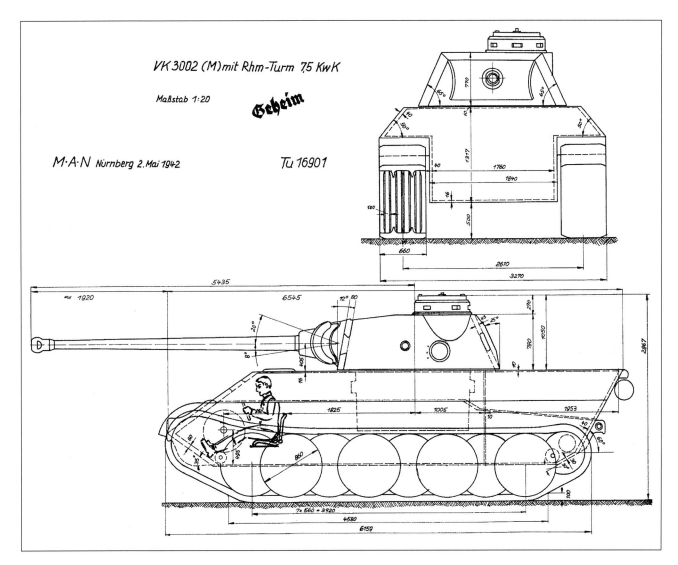

VK 3002 (M) mit Rhm-Turm 7,5 KwK

Maßstab 1:20

Geheim

M·A·N Nürnberg 2. Mai 1942

Tu 16901

the former, the MAN design had a range of 75km greater than the DB design and when travelling across country this approximated to some 55km more.

■ The wider hull also permitted greater area for the fighting compartment – 7.26m² compared to that the DB's 6.43m². The space within the fighting compartment had been sized by MAN for a man of average stature – that is of 1.70m – thus any 'extra' working space would be beneficial to a crew of five men, although by no means could that of the production Panther be described as excessive.

■ It had a lower ground pressure than the DB machine which was 0.20bar higher than that of the MAN Panther, which itself was just 0.02bar higher than that of the T-34 at 0.68, even though it was heavier than the Russian design.

■ The track width of the MAN design was also wider than that of the DB design – with the latter's being some 120mm less than that of the MAN. Although not excessive, the combination of the lower ground pressure/ wider tracks meant that the Panther would have a much superior ground 'footprint' (especially across rough terrain) than any existing German tank, and would enable it to cover ground that the T-34 could but which had proven impassable for the Panzers III and IV in Russia.

■ Although both designs were to employ the same 75mm KwK (*Kampfwagenkanone*) 42 L/70 main gun, the DB proposal required the development of a new turret and this could not have been ready before December 1942 at the earliest. It was the case that the DB turret was also rejected by the commission on

ABOVE This basic plan was presented to the commission that had been set up by Hitler to examine both the MAN and DB proposals for the new medium tank for the German Army.

other grounds. The MAN Panther would utilise a pre-existing turret originally designed by RM of Düsseldorf for installation on the Tiger I heavy tank, when it was possible that it might mount the 75mm L/70 (before the design was finalised on the turret designed by Krupp to carry the 88mm L/56 weapon. Furthermore, the turret ring of the DB design was 50mm less than that of the MAN proposal and even with DB's own turret proposal having been rejected, it could not mount the RM-designed turret. Furthermore, the fitting of the 75mm main gun would have required modification to fit the DB turret even had it gone ahead. The time required to address these matters could not be borne, given the urgency attached to getting production started on the new design by the end of 1942.

■ It was also pointed out that the manner in which the motor compartment of the MAN Panther was isolated in the rear of the hull would permit this design to make passage across water obstacles without extensive preparation. The original specification had laid down that this should be 4m of water. However, in practice on production machines this facility was never uniformly provided for.

Between the date of the award of the contract to MAN and the end of 1942, the development of the new medium tank carried on apace. In the days following the award for the new medium tank, Wa Prüf 6 granted MAN contracts to produce two experimental Panthers (*Versuchsfahrgestelle*), with the first being for a working chassis sans turret to be produced by August, and the second for a chassis mounting an RM-supplied turret and armament, to be ready for testing in September 1942. Oberbaurat Kniepkamp spent much time at MAN during the course of the construction of these two pilot vehicles, overseeing the fitting of the new double torsion bar suspension. The hulls of both examples were constructed of mild steel and were fitted out with many features that did not see their way on to production machines. For example, neither was constructed utilising interlocking joints and the road wheels had 18 rim bolts.

Even as MAN turned to the construction of the two *Versuchsfahrgestelle* in the days after the award of the contract on 15 May, just four days later a major conference chaired by Albert Speer set about the allocation of Panther production to other manufacturers. Such was the priority and importance of this tank that production was spread, in a rolling programme, across four of the main tank manufacturers in the Reich. In all cases, this required a major programme of tooling-up and the creation of new production lines, as well as the very rapid identification of sub-contractors to supply the

BELOW AND OPPOSITE The first two MAN *Versuchs-Panther* (Nos V1 and V2) emerged in the autumn of 1943. Both were of soft steel of which only the second was fitted with a turret.

myriad fittings that would be required. This in itself is testimony to the remarkable speed with which this whole project now moved forward. Overhanging the 19 May meeting was the knowledge that Hitler required that at least 250 Panthers be available for the 1943 summer offensive in Russia. As an aside, this of itself is interesting. The German 1942 summer offensive did not begin until 22 June and Hitler had stressed that this had to bring about the collapse of the Soviet Union in that year. It would seem that notwithstanding what was being said on this matter, to specify as he did that the Panther be available for the 1943 summer offensive, suggests that he did not really believe that Russia would be defeated in 1942. DB was instructed to begin tooling-up so as to start construction and production of the MAN design alongside that of the parent company before the end of 1942, although neither company produced their first machines until January and February 1943 respectively. Two other companies, notably Maschinenfabrik Niedersachsen-Hannover (MNH) and Henschel of Kassel were told to prepare their factories for production of the Panther beginning in July 1943, although in actuality both began earlier with the former producing its first in February and the latter in March 1943. Even then, in the light of Hitler's continuing requirement that the requisite numbers of Panthers be available for

the 1943 summer offensive, these demands were changed in fairly rapid order. Such was the urgency of the Panther programme that it:

> . . . was placed in the same category of urgency as oil and locomotive production programmes. Greater pressure was brought to bear on all the firms involved in order to unconditionally meet the demands of Hitler.

Given that all four companies were also still involved in the production of the Panzer III, and in the case of Henschel, also gearing up for the production of the Tiger I, the demands made on these manufacturers and of all the satellite companies providing equipment for these tanks was very great and was to lead to bottlenecks that were to impact on the production schedule.

Nonetheless, by the end of 1942, an advanced medium panzer that at the start of the year was just a specification on paper, was about to enter production. The design, testing of prototypes, and achievement of first production in the opening months of 1943 was a remarkable feat. What was to emerge was what many still acknowledge as the finest medium tank of the Second World War. But the rapidity of its creation would also bring problems in its train, some of which would not be eliminated before the war ended in defeat just two and a half years later.

Chapter Two

Production of the Panther and its variants

During the course of it production life, which lasted from January 1943 through to April 1945, the Panther medium tank appeared in three iterations, namely the Ausf D, A and G. This chapter looks at the external differences of these as well as providing a coverage of the Bergepanther recovery vehicle and the Jagdpanther tank destroyer.

OPPOSITE An overhead shot of the production lines at MIAG, the principal manufacturer of the Jagdpanther. In total, 419 were built through to March 1945.

Production of the Panther

The very speed with which the whole Panther programme was now proceeding brought problems for the companies tooling-up to produce it. A great number of novel items had to be manufactured from scratch, even though many others were supplied from already-available items. The special status of the Panther programme had been restated at a meeting on 17 December 1942 when it was stressed how urgent it was. However, in spite of the exhortations to proceed as rapidly as possible, the considerable complexity of the

programme – not just for the main contractors but also for the many subcontractors – saw the early schedule slip with MAN stating it could not deliver the first four Panthers by the end of December 1942, as had been previously agreed. These were instead handed over the following month.

MAN delivered eleven, DB six and MNH just one in February. It was only in March that all four companies involved in the production programme started delivering new-build machines in any number, with 75 being produced in that month with numbers in April being just 84, with none from MAN.

Images of the MAN production line mirror the scenes found at DB, Henschel, MNH and Demag (Demag began Panther production with the Ausf A) between March and the end of the war, although of course by then many of these factories had been repeatedly targeted by the USAAF and the RAF. That being said, the highest monthly production figure for Panthers was 155 by MAN in 1944.

The sequence of pictures below serves to convoy an impression of the Panther production line at the MAN factory in Nuremberg. These images were taken on 16 March 1943 inside building No M24.

OPPOSITE AND ABOVE Although the general shape of the design is recognisably that of a Panther, there are a number of features that were unique to the V2. It has the same globular muzzle brake as fitted to the Panzer IV F2, the protruding commander's cupola and the singular large exhaust fitted to the rear of the hull.

Panther variants: part one

This section addresses the (primarily) external differences between each variant of the Panther Ausf D, A and G. The second section covers the Panzerbefehlswagen Panther and the late war infra-red-equipped Panthers. The third

ABOVE Production of the new Panther was a few months late in beginning at MAN. Seen here is the specially developed large machine tool created to drill out the holes in the Panther hull for the suspension and drive. This machine was duplicated in those other factories building the Panther and Jagdpanther. *(All this spread NARA)*

RIGHT One of the production lines at MAN shows the hulls having already received some or all of their torsion bars, while on its other side are a number of Panther hulls with turrets supplied by RM having just been assembled.

232609

ABOVE The Panther's transmission, designed by Zahnradfabrik Friedrichshafen, along with its steering gear, are seen being assembled by MAN workers and one seconded Panzer crewman.

LEFT In this photograph, taken in Hall M24 at the MAN factory, the Panther hulls have moved along the production line and have been fitted with their drive and road wheels.

ABOVE The hulls have had their road wheels and rear idlers fitted, although they are without the drive sprockets. The boxes attached to the sides of the hull are temporary fittings to hold the tools of the technicians working on the upper hull. *(NARA)*

LEFT A similar scene at the Henschel factory. The picture was taken in June 1943. This company produced its first Panthers in March that year. *(NARA)*

section addresses the Bergepanther (recovery Panther) and Jagdpanther tank destroyer.

Each Panther built was allocated a Fahrgestellnummer (Fgst.Nr) or chassis number.

Panther Ausf D (Sd.Kfz. 171)

The speed at which production of the first Panther began at the companies contracted to do so was remarkably quick. Trials of the two Panther prototypes were concluded before the end of 1942. The whole process of production that followed was highly complex and the level of co-ordination required to ensure the mass of sub-contracted parts were produced to the appropriate standard and despatched to the participating factories required a high degree of supervision. It has been noted elsewhere that:

> . . . it would be wrong to describe the MAN plant in Nurnberg, Henschel at Kassel, Demag at Berlin-Albrechtshof, Daimler-

Benz at Hannover-Linden as Panzer manufacturers. They did indeed produce Panzers but they would best be described as assembly firms. The production of Panzers involved numerous companies and organisations from the design of the vehicle to its series production. The majority of the components were sourced from specialist sub-contractors and would then be assembled by the main assembly firms.

Overseeing the assembly process was rigorous but, even then, the first Ausf Ds off the production line were late. The speed with which the new medium panzer had been produced accounts for so many of the initial technical problems experienced with it. The Ausf D evidenced most trouble with the fuel lines and final drives – indeed the latter issue would never be resolved before the war's end. Such were the teething problems with the new machine; a consequence of the very little time that had been made available for testing the Panther before it found its way to service. In truth, the Ausf D came to be viewed as a development series.

Ausf D		
Number produced: 842 between January and September 1943		
Manufacturer	**Fgst.Nr**	**Number built**
MAN	210001–210254	**242**
Daimler-Benz	211006–211250	**250**
MNH	213001–213220	**220**
Henschel	212010–212130	**130**
Weight: 43 tons		

Note: There was not always an exact correlation between Fgst.Nrs and numbers produced, hence the apparent discrepancies.

Identifying features:

1) Drum cupola with six direct-vision open ports (not periscopes).
2) Letterbox flap for the MG on the right side of the glacis.
3) From April 1943 weld brackets added to underside of panniers to take *Schürzen* (protective armoured plates) on the hull side.
4) Beginning in May 1943 all Panthers built with the HL 210P30 engine had this replaced by the HL 230P30 engine employing a cast-iron block.
5) 16 bolts on the wheel discs. From June 1943 an additional bolt was added between each of the 16 rim bolts.

BELOW Panther Ausf D turret before modification.

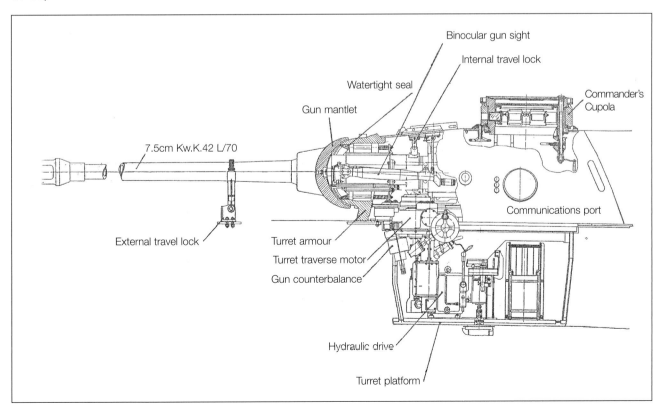

7.5cm Kw.K.42 L/70

External travel lock

Gun mantlet

Watertight seal

Binocular gun sight

Internal travel lock

Commander's Cupola

Communications port

Turret armour

Turret traverse motor

Gun counterbalance

Hydraulic drive

Turret platform

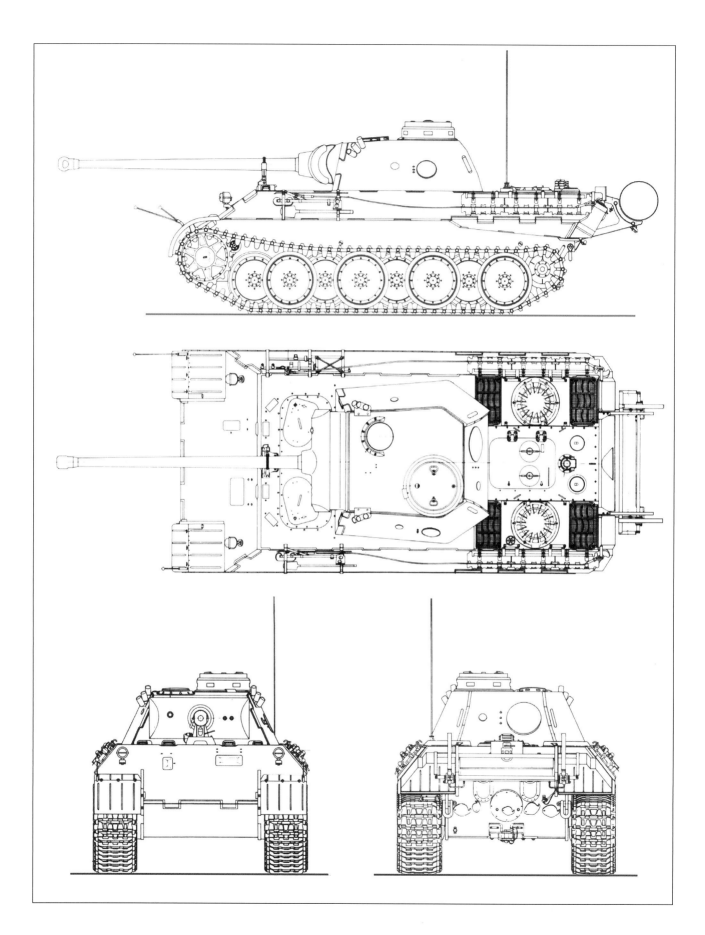

OPPOSITE PAGE This three-view drawing of the Panther Ausf D, the designation of the first production model, illustrates the manner in which the design has changed over that of the V2 prototype. Note that the fuel tank carried on the rear hull was never fitted in actuality. These images are sometimes mistakenly labelled as the Ausf A.

6) Pistol ports on either side of the turret were discontinued from June 1943.
7) On the left side of the turret there was a communications hatch. This was discontinued in July 1943.
8) In June 1943 a ring mount for a *Fliegerbeschussgerät* – an anti-aircraft gun mount to carry an MG 34 – was added to the cupola.
9) Smoke candle dischargers – albeit only on early production models. These were discontinued from June 1943.
10) Two front headlights were fitted until July

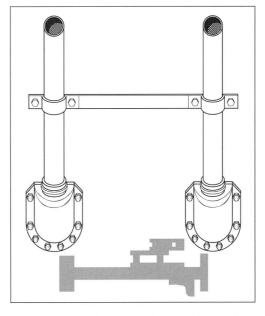

1943, from when on only a single example was fitted on the right side of the glacis.
11) Rain guard fitted above the gunsight holes in the mantlet.

LEFT Panther Ausf D exhaust. *(Mark Rolfe)*

BELOW The Ausf D remained in production from January through September 1943, with 842 being built.

Even as the German leader had consented that the MAN proposal for the new Panther medium tank be accepted for production, he had voiced his doubts that the design was sufficiently armoured enough to cope with the near future battlefield. In consequence, and even before the Ausf A entered production in January 1943, discussions had been under way for the Panther's replacement. This was referred to initially as the Panther 2, and, after April 1943, the Panther II. The original Panther was designated as the Panther I.

Although it was not envisaged that the armament would be changed, there was however to be a significant 'upgrading' of the new design's armour protection to both the turret and the hull. The glacis was to be increased to 100mm and the hull sides to 60mm, as was the turret front which was to be increased to 100mm and the turret sides to 60mm. At the time of its design, the Panther II was envisaged as weighing some 47 tons. The engine was to remain the same as for the Panther I, as was the transmission and all other aspects of the original design. It is likely that by the time it had entered service (had it done so)

the Panther II would have weighed in at nearer 50 tons. This much more heavily armoured German medium tank would thus have weighed 6 tons more than the Soviet JS-II heavy tank that went into service in 1944!

In January 1943, just as the very first Panther I Ausf Ds were leaving the production line at DB, the decision was taken to start Panther II production just nine months hence – in September 1943 – with the initial example to be produced by the Demag company. The four companies producing the Panther I were instructed to continue with its production through to 1944. They would only shift over to production of the Panther II at the end of 1944. Other companies, namely Krupp-Gruson, Nibelungenwerk and Werk-Falkensee were earmarked to begin production of the Panther II at various times in 1943 and 1944.

Just a month later matters became more complex when the decision was taken to harmonise aspects of the design of what was to become the Tiger 3 (later Tiger II) and the Panther 2. They were to be equipped with the same transmission, motor and steel-tyred road wheels. The Tiger II was to have a suspension of nine road wheels per side and the Panther II would have seven. The Panther II was also to employ the same single torsion bar suspension as on the Tiger II. The tracks for the Panther II were adopted to be used as the transport tracks for the Tiger II. Although a series of other modifications to the design of the Panther II were proposed as early as May 1943, enthusiasm for the whole project had gone off the boil and indeed the development of the Panther II was suspended, with production of the Panther I to continue for the foreseeable future. In part, this was due to the success of the thin *Schürzen* plates added to the hull of the Panther I, which to a certain extent negated the problem of weak side armour.

However, aspects of the Panther II would find their way on to the Panther Ausf G. Only one experimental Panther II chassis was actually produced, this surviving the war and being shipped back to the United States 'wearing' a Panther Ausf G turret. It is at present to be found in a restored state and on display at the Patton Museum.

BELOW Only a single Panther II chassis was completed by MAN before the project was cancelled. It never received a turret for the same reason.

12) From November 1943 Zimmerit anti-magnetic mine paste (see separate box on page 39) applied to Panther Ausf Ds that did not have it added at the assembly plants. Ausf Ds first had Zimmerit applied from September 1943 at factories.

A whole series of smaller changes were introduced that primarily affected the internals of the machine.

Panther Ausf A (Sd.Kfz. 171)

The process that led to the decision to 'upgrade' the Panther Ausf D began even as the first examples of that model left the production line at MAN in February 1943. It was, however, one that was confined to a discussion in the first instance between Wa Prüf 6 and the manufacturer of the turret and its armament, Rheinmetall-Borsig. Although

ABOVE This excellent close-up image of the turret and front hull of a Panther Ausf D, captured by the Russians at Kursk, gives us a clear view of the tool rack and the three of six smoke dischargers carried on the front of either side of the turret.

LEFT Replete in full colour is this image of the running Panther Ausf A that belongs to the Panzer Museum at Münster in Germany.

there were as yet no combat reports to draw upon, it was apparent from the testing of the first examples of the new panzer that in order to ensure that its core element – its armament – could be employed to its maximum effectiveness, a number of changes would be required to be introduced.

It was, however, a matter of absolute priority to get the Ausf D into production and to build up not only enough machines to satisfy the Führer's demand to have the 250 earmarked for the forthcoming summer offensive in Russia, but also to permit the conversion of as many Army and Waffen SS battalions as possible to the new machine. Whether or not there were those in Germany who realised that the war was already lost was beside the point, for under Albert Speer, the German war economy was undergoing a belated, massive expansion. And with Guderian's appointment to the newly created and independent post of Inspector General of Panzer Troops, armed with a brief from Hitler to rebuild the *Panzerwaffe* into a war-winning weapon also in that same month, the importance of the Panther became such that any changes would have to be incremental and not radical, as the critical factor was one of output. Any interruption of the production lines could not be countenanced.

Confined to improvements to the turret alone, notwithstanding known flaws in the suspension and drive train that had emerged in testing, Wa Prüf 6 and RM began discussions as to how to address weaknesses in the turret design of the Panther. But even at this early date it was recognised that such changes would be planned for introduction at a particular point in the production line and with as little dislocation to production as possible. The first discussion between the two bodies on this matter took place on 18 February, even as design work was continuing on the Panther 2. Out of it flowed the decision to implement changes to the turret that would be introduced once the 851st Ausf D had been produced. That would provide ample time for all of the manufacturing companies involved in Panther manufacture to be prepared for the necessary changes to the hull of the Ausf D to accommodate the new turret. All work on the new turret and its production would be carried out by RM, and these turrets, as was already happening with the Ausf D, would be shipped by rail to the production companies.

There was to be no change to the basic dimensions and design of the Ausf D turret. Those changes that were to occur affected the turret roof and the turret mantlet. On the turret roof a periscope was allocated for the loader who, on the Ausf D, had been 'blind' – having no facility to see what was going on outside the turret. Of greatest importance for this part of the tank was the introduction of a new cast cupola for the tank commander; this was to be fitted with seven periscopes. It had been recognised quite early on that the drum type of cupola of the Ausf A was not the most effective design. The cast cupola provided greater protection and was also fitted with a ring which was welded to the armoured cowlings of the periscopes. The ring also permitted the attachment of a *Fliegerbeschussgerät* – an anti-aircraft machine-gun mount to carry an MG 34. This was not standard and many Ausf As were seen in service without this fitting. It was necessary for the purposes of fitting the new cupola to change the method of joining the turret armour. This saw the shift from dovetailed interlocks to parallel interlocks.

The requirement for new waterproof seals had seen the need for the creation of an alternative casting for the turret front plate and the trunnion armour. The latter now acquired a distinctive shape that was to hold through to the Ausf G and these were characterised by having dish-shaped, convex bulges (these can be seen in detail in Chapter 4, see page 95).

The introduction of a new turret race on the Ausf A precluded it from taking a turret from the earlier model. Indeed, it has been noted elsewhere that very little photographic or documentary evidence has emerged since 1945 to show that this happened – except in three rare cases – and even then it is uncertain whether these were actually operational.

It was certainly not a procedure adopted by Seibert-Stalhau of Aschaffenburg, who were contracted to renovate damaged returned Panther chassis. In the case of the Ausf D and later early Ausf As received by the company, many were rebuilt and then employed as the basis of Bergepanthers.

The turrets made surplus by this process were then modified and employed for use as fixed-turret defence positions. These were encountered in some numbers by Allied troops in Italy and a photograph exists of one that was employed astride a road intersection in Berlin in May 1945.

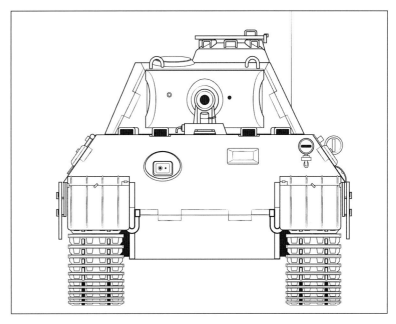

Ausf A		
Number produced: 2,200 produced between August 1943 and July 1944		
Manufacturer	**Fgst.Nr**	**Number built**
MAN	210255–210899	**645**
Daimler-Benz	151901–152575	**675**
MNH	154801–155630	**830**
Demag	158101–158150	**50**
Weight: 44.8 tons		

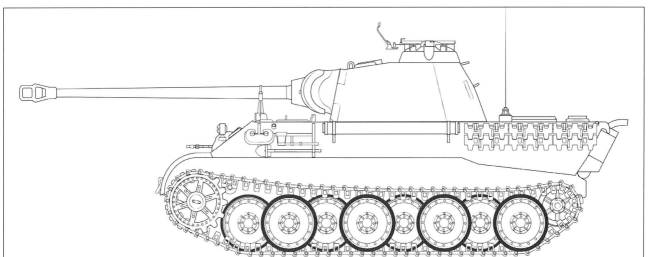

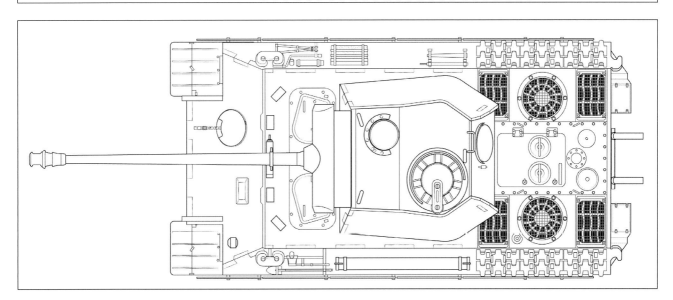

Identifying features:

While the Ausf A chassis remained the same as that of its predecessor, from September 1943 it was fitted with a new and improved turret (see three-view drawing and caption of Ausf A for more detail and explanation).

1) Cast cupola with seven periscopes, each protected with armoured covers. A sighting vane and its mounting bracket fitted to the new cupola. Retained on the Ausf G. A ring on the cupola welded to the armoured covers. On this could be added a mount for the carriage of an MG 34.

2) Gradual replacement of road wheels with 16 bolts by ones with 24 rim bolts once the supply of the former was exhausted.

3) From late November/early December 1943 the flap on the glacis was replaced with a ball mount for an MG 34 used by the radio operator.

4) At the same time the binocular *Turmzielfernrohr* 12 (TZF) gunsight was replaced by the monocular TZF 12a gunsight.

5) In November 1943, the HL 230P30 motor was set at the factory to an output reduced to 2,500rpm with corresponding reduction in top speed to 28mph.

6) In January 1944, pistol ports on turret sides discontinued.

7) In March 1944, a *Nahverteidigungswaffe* (close-defence weapon) was fitted to the roof of the turret. It was fixed in elevation at 50 degrees but could rotate through 36 degrees.

8) Zimmerit anti-magnetic mine coating was added from September 1943.

9) During the course of its production life twin cooling pipes for the left engine exhaust manifold were mounted in parallel with the left exhaust pipe (see diagram).

10) Between November and December 1943, a towing coupling derived from the Bergepanther fitting was added to lower hull of the Panther. It was discontinued in December.

11) The jack moved from a horizontal position below the exhaust system to a vertical position between the pipes of the exhaust system.

ZIMMERIT

On the assumption that the Red Army and Allied armies would begin to field magnetic anti-tank mines that could be emplaced on a tank in the same fashion as the German HHL-3 magnetic grenade, the Berlin company of C.W. Zimmer developed a paste that could be applied to panzers to counter their effectiveness. It worked on the simple principle of creating a barrier between the metal of the panzer and the enemy magnetic mine. It was thus a form of stand-off protection, albeit chemical in nature, rather than metal, as in the case of *Schürzen*. It was applied to all panzers and assault guns in production at the time and subsequently to many in the field. It was first applied to the Panther from September 1943. The paste was constituted of the five following materials:

1) Barium sulphate – 40%
2) Polyvinyl acetate – 25%
3) Ochre pigment – 15%
4) Zinc sulphide – 10%
5) Sawdust – 10%.

Although each of the companies building the Panther applied Zimmerit on the production lines of all new-build Panthers during the time it was mandated to be applied – that is, between September 1943 and 9 September 1944 – the manner in which they finished it was not set down so that there was a uniform pattern. Rather, the companies were left to adopt their own methods of finishing off the paste with a pattern inscribed into it.

However, not all companies applied the material from the outset when the order to do so was issued. Whereas MAN complied in September 1943, DB commenced in October, MNH in late September/October and Demag in September. The manner in which each company did so became a feature which gives a clue as to the Panther's factory of manufacture.

Once the paste was applied at the factory, a drying time of between three to six days was then required for it to harden off. The amount of time required was dependent upon contingencies such as the season of application, the temperature in the factory and its humidity. In some cases a blowtorch was employed to help speed up the process. For some authors Zimmerit has become a subject in its own right and the bibliography will highlight those books that the reader can consult for more information. This is especially well covered in the late Roddy MacDougall and Martin Block's excellent book: *Panther: External Appearance and Design Changes*.

In the end, the concern that motivated its application did not come to pass as none of those armies fighting the Germans ended up employing magnetic mines in any number. Nor did they emulate the general application of a Zimmerit analogue, although the British Army did some experiments to explore the notion.

The decision to terminate the application of Zimmerit was governed by claims that the coating had itself caught fire on occasions, thus endangering the tank, as well as the aforementioned point that the enemy had not deployed magnetic mines in quantity. It was also the case that application of Zimmerit on the production line and the time it took to dry out was therefore deemed to be wasteful and was discontinued.

BELOW Zimmerit paste has been applied to the glacis of this Panther Ausf A. It will be added in turn to the hull sides, the hull rear and the turret sides and mantlet. Zimmerit was first ordered to be applied to all new-build panzers in September 1943.

RIGHT Panther Ausf A exhaust schematics.
(Mark Rolfe)

1 *Ausf A, Type 1.*
2 *Ausf A, Type 2.*
3 *Ausf A, Type 3.*
4 *Ausf A, Type 4.*
5 *Ausf A, Type 5.*

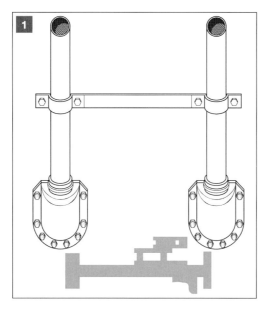

12) From February 1944, changes to the fittings on the rear plate of the Panther were introduced.
13) An improved hydraulic turret traverse was introduced, which slaved the speed of the turret traverse to engine speed. This meant that at the maximum permissible engine speed of 3,000rpm the turret could be traversed 360 degrees in 15 seconds. The de-rating of the engine speed in November 1943 to 2,500rpm therefore impacted upon the speed of the turret traverse.
14) A *Kampfraumheizung* (crew compartment heater) was provided for the Ausf A beginning in January 1944.

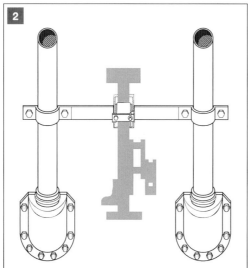

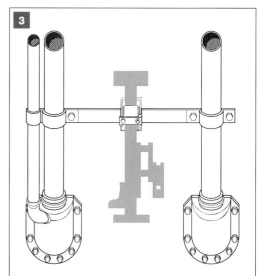

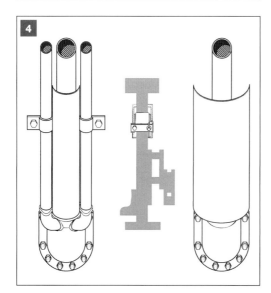

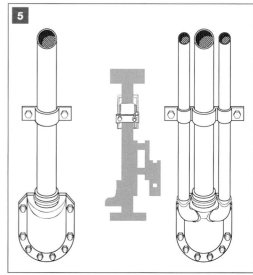

233129

Panther Ausf G (Sd.Kfz. 171)

Just four months after the decision was taken to introduce the Ausf A after the production of the 851st Ausf D, it was decided in a meeting at MAN to embark upon a much more significant upgrade of the Panther. This flowed from the decision that as the Panther I was to remain in production for the foreseeable future, it made sense to incorporate some of the design features of the then still proposed Panther II to render it a more effective machine. These changes would also make the new version simpler to produce.

MAN was the lead company responsible for this upgrade, which would see the focus on this occasion directed not towards the turret,

but to the hull. The changes introduced to the turret on the Ausf A would remain more or less the same for the new mark, save for a few modifications. Thus the Panther Ausf G would inherit the turret of the Ausf A *in toto*. Such were the scale of changes to the hull that it was, to all intents and purposes, a new, albeit simplified, hull design, although retaining a strong similarity to the earlier two variants.

There was no change to the suspension, it being identical to that of the Ausf A. There were changes to the floor of the hull, but the most noticeable difference was the shape of the hull side/pannier. The wedge shape seen on the two previous marks was dispensed with and the new shape of the pannier floor

ABOVE In this three-photograph sequence of a production Ausf A built by MAN, this Panther is wearing full Zimmerit and has a machine-gun mount attached to its cupola ring.

be found in the relevant table in Chapter 3 (see page 64).

The changes most noticeable to the crew applied to the driver and radio operator. The hatches above their heads in the previous two versions of the Panther were replaced on the Ausf G from a lift and swivel hatch to a lift and raise hatch. These new hatches were both easier to manufacture and cheaper to produce. In May 1944, MAN began fitting jettisonable versions of these hatches. Gone also was the vision slit in the glacis for the driver, to be replaced by a rotating periscope mounted in the roof, in front of the driver's head. The only protuberance on the glacis was now the bulge that housed the ball mount for the hull machine gun.

Unlike with the introduction of the Ausf A – when it had been possible to harmonise a collective change to the new machine on the production lines of all the companies producing the Panther – by March 1944, when production started at MAN, the war situation no longer permitted such to take place. German industrial sites were by that date becoming regular targets for the USAAF by day and the RAF by night, although it was the former that focused on primarily industrial targets. As the number of

ABOVE The two extremes of the Wehrmacht on the Eastern Front in about 1944 – a Panther G, the most modern tank in the world – while in the foreground is a Russian *panje* cart evacuating German troops westward in retreat.

would see it follow a straight line from the point at which it started at the front of the hull through to the rear of the hull at the forward outer edge of the radiator assembly. This changed the angle of the upper side wall from 40 degrees in the Ausf D and Ausf A, to 29 degrees, albeit with an increase in its thickness from 40mm to 50mm. Other changes to the thicknesses of the armour of the new hull can

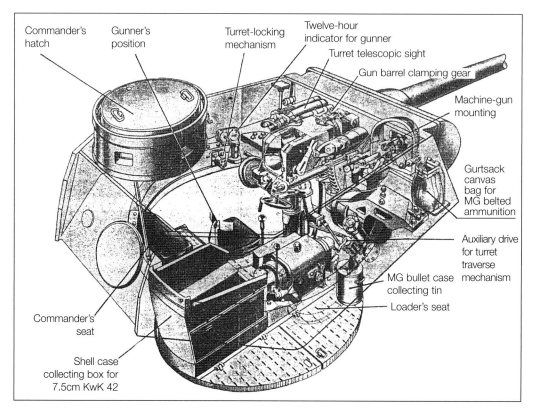

Commander's hatch

Gunner's position

Turret-locking mechanism

Twelve-hour indicator for gunner

Turret telescopic sight

Gun barrel clamping gear

Machine-gun mounting

Gurtsack canvas bag for MG belted ammunition

Auxiliary drive for turret traverse mechanism

MG bullet case collecting tin

Loader's seat

Commander's seat

Shell case collecting box for 7.5cm KwK 42

RIGHT Panther Ausf D turret.

Panther Ausf G.
(Mark Rolfe)

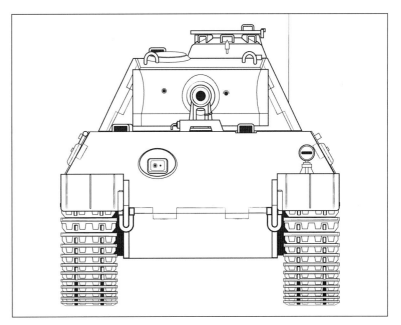

targets attacked increased, the smooth supply of the many components needed to furnish the Panther production lines became more problematic. In consequence, the decision was taken to stagger the introduction of the Ausf G by the three companies now involved in the production of the panzer. MAN produced its first Ausf G with a *Fahrgestellnummer* of 120301 in March 1944, to be followed by DB in May and finally MNH in Hannover in July. Despite the impact of Allied bombing during 1944, which was growing in strength, Panther production in that year reached a grand total of 3,777 machines, of which the bulk were Ausf Gs.

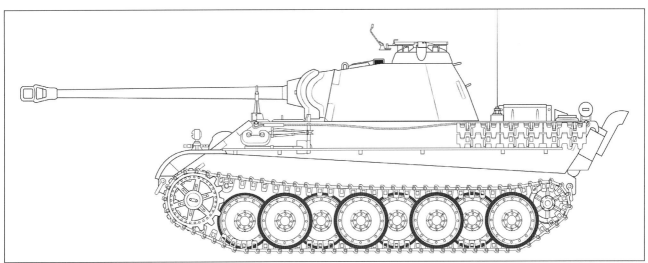

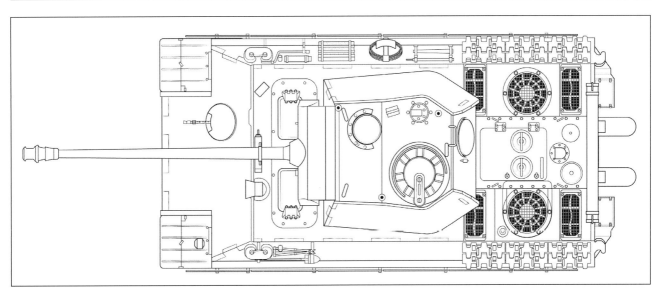

In September 1944, MAN completed about 20 Panther Ausf Gs with steel-tyred road wheels – the same as those employed on the Tiger I and II. A number of these were employed and lost in combat.

Ausf G
Number produced: 2,953 between March 1944 and April 1945

Manufacturer	Fgst.Nr	Number built
MAN	120301–121443	**1,143**
Daimler-Benz	124301–125304	**1,004**
MNH	128301–129114	**806**
Weight: 45.5 tons		

Identifying features:

1) Redesigned side sloping armour with armour thickness raised to 50mm.
2) In September 1944 the addition of the Zimmerit coating was ordered to be discontinued.
3) All Panthers produced after 7 September 1944 no longer carried Zimmerit.
4) Deletion of the driver's glacis visor.
5) Fitting of a new traversable periscope for the driver.
6) Introduction of new jettisonable hatches on the hull roof for the radio operator and driver.
7) Three threaded sockets were added to the turret roof to accept the fitting of a 2-ton jib boom – *Behelfskran* (see Chapter 4, page 96-7).
8) A new ventilator cover was added beneath the main gun lock.

9) The single headlight was shifted from the glacis (as on the Ausf A) to the mudguard on the Ausf G.

10) Ammunition stowage was increased to 82 main rounds.

11) A sheet metal rain guard was added over the driver's periscope.

12) Beginning in May 1944, the cast armoured protectors that covered the base of the exhaust pipes were replaced by square welded, armoured box-shaped guards.

13) In August 1944, a sheet metal cover running the length of the top of the mantlet was introduced to stop debris falling in between the gap behind it.

14) The exhaust pipes on the rear plate were protected by welded-on armoured guards. In June 1944, sheet metal cowls were provided to decrease the bright glow of the very hot exhaust pipes at night.

15) From September 1944, a small number of Panthers were equipped with infra-red searchlights.

16) Again in September 1944, a small number of Panthers were fitted with steel-tyred road wheels, as employed on the Tigers I and II. The initial installation was on Panther 121052.

17) In the same month a sheet metal rain guard was provided to stop water falling on the gunsight opening on the mantlet.

18) In October 1944, all companies building the Panther (except DB, which retained the old design) began fitting a new, larger, self-cleaning idler wheel.

19) In October, *Flammvernichter* mufflers were fitted to prevent glow from exhaust outlets showing at night.

20) In the same month a crew compartment heater was introduced. Can be recognised by raised cover emplaced over the cooling air outlet (see walk-around)

21) Introduction of thickened gun mantlet to prevent deflection of enemy shells into the top of the hull where driver/radio operator sat.

22) *Schürzen* now hung from a permanently attached runner extending the length of hull side.

23) Only change from the turret of the Ausf A to that of the Ausf G was the attachment of a welded brace to the rear lifting point.

24) All Ausf Gs fitted to take *Nahverteidigungswaffe* (close defence weapon).

25) The small rubber-tyred wheel behind the drive sprocket was replaced with a solid metal skid shoe (this can be seen on the Bovington Panther in Chapter 4, see page 110.)

Primary change: A redesigned chassis which included a new hull. The sloping side armour was redesigned and made thicker – from 40mm to 50mm – and set at a different angle. On the Ausf A this was 30 degrees and on the Ausf G it was changed to 40 degrees. Forward belly plate also increased by 5mm. The Ausf G employed the same turret as the Ausf A.

LEFT A very late Ausf G, manufactured in December 1944, wears the steel chin extension added to the lower gun mantlet to prevent the deflection of cncmy shclls into the roof of the hull where the driver and radio operator sat.

BELOW The *Schmalturm* for the proposed Ausf F Panther that never went into production. This particular turret was acquired by the British Army after the war and returned to the UK for analysis.

As part of the OKH-led improvement programme for the Panther established in late 1944, DB had been charged with the creation and production of a new turret. DB co-operated with Rheinmetall on this venture. MAN, the design parent for the concept and chassis of the Panther, was not involved. When interviewed at the end of the war, Dr Wiebecke claimed that MAN personnel knew little of the details of the turret.

The OKH specification required:

1) A reduction in turret frontal area without

reducing the space in the turret for the crew to operate.
2) Elimination of the shot trap found on the early variants of the Panther.
3) Installation of a stereoscopic rangefinder.
4) Substitution of a co-axial MG 42 in place of the MG 34.
5) Built with the capability of being converted to a Panzerbefehlswagen Panther (a night-fighting Panther) with infra-red equipment.
6) It was also stated that the new turret had to be cheaper to produce; 30–40% fewer man hours to produce was the requirement.

The *Schmalturm* (small turret), for what was intended to be the next variant of the Panther – the Ausf F – was what emerged to address the specification. It can be seen from the accompanying images how much smaller dimensionally the new turret was externally, even though the turret ring remained the same. The shape was derived from that of the production (Henschel) model of the turret of the Tiger II, albeit with the bustle eliminated. It received the designation Gerät 710 ('Schmal

The production status of the Panther and the Emergency Panzer Programme of January 1945

Under the Emergency Panzer Programme of January 1945, there was an attempt to try to bring about some semblance of order from the wreckage of the *Panzerwaffe* with a final reorganisation of that arm. This saw a radical paring back of the number of tank types to remain in production and one of those slated for cancellation was the Panther. Just 275 were to be produced in February and 290 in March and April, with all production being halted in May – which is what happened in actuality, due to Allied troops occupying the factories they were built in by that date. As we have noted elsewhere, production of the Jagdpanther was due to end in that month also.

Panther variants: part two

Panzerbefehlswagen (Pz.Bef.Wg) Panther

Out of the total Panther production between January 1943 and the last manufactured in April 1945, 329 had been modified on the MAN production line to become Panzerbefehlswagen (command tanks). Only MAN was contracted to produce this variant, it being distinguished from the standard Panther only by the inclusion of additional radio equipment to enable the commander to exercise control over his unit. The external differences that permitted the command Panther to be distinguished from the standard Panther lay in the number of extra radio aerials carried by the former.

The Pz.Bef.Wg was allocated one of two distinctive designations – either Sd.Kfz. 267 or Sd.Kfz. 268 – dependent upon the radio fit of the vehicle concerned. As with the standard Panther, all command Panthers were fitted

Turm 605'). Frontal armour of the new design was increased by 10mm to 120mm, which was in turn given a greater slope, going from 11 degrees to 20 degrees. In order to eliminate the shot trap caused by the wide mantlet of the earlier Panther, a new and thicker-cast armoured-type mantlet of 120 degrees, shaped as a *Saukopfblend* and similar to that used on the Henschel turret Tiger II, was designed. The thickness of the turret armour was also raised by an extra 15mm at the same angle of 25 degrees. Changes to the design of the gun (*ie* the buffer and recuperator) were now mounted underneath, rather to the side of the barrel. The gunsight was to be the TZF 13, fixed to the left side of the gun cradle. No muzzle brake was to be fitted, albeit a number of early guns were equipped with such. These changes led to a new designation for the weapon, which became the 75mm KwK44/1. In addition, the episcope for the loader was eliminated and a new, redesigned lower cupola was to be fitted.

The war ended before the *Schmalturm* could be placed in production, although one of the prototype turrets was placed on an Ausf G

ABOVE This is what remains of the *Schmalturm* seen opposite. It was used for firing tests by the British Army after the war – hence the damage. It was rescued and then placed inside the Tank Museum at Bovington, where it is on display.

chassis and trialled at the testing ground at Kummersdorf.

Examples of the few *Schmalturme* built were taken both to the UK and USA. The remains of one can be seen at the Tank Museum at Bovington in the UK.

LEFT
Panzerbefehlswagen Panther Ausf D entrained for the Eastern Front. The upper part of the star antenna is visible, as is the aerial on the roof of the turret in the foreground. The camo can be seen mounted on the roof of the Panther in the background.

LEFT A very clear image of the mantlet and cupola of a Panzerbefehlswagen Panther Ausf A. It is wearing Zimmerit. The machine-gun aperture on the mantlet is stoppered up and there is a rain guard over the two periscope holes to the right of the main gun. The top of the star antenna is visible behind the tank commander.

with the FuG 5 radio set, but unlike in the standard Panther, it was not located in the hull above the transmission, but on the right-hand side of the turret in both variants, with the transformers necessary to permit the FuG 5 to work employing the space normally occupied by the co-axial machine gun. The redundant hole in the mantlet from which the barrel normally projected was sealed by an armoured plug. The 2m-tall *Stabantenne* (rod aerial) needed to service the FuG 5 was located in an *Antennenfuss* (antenna foot) on the rear right-hand side of the turret roof.

In order to generate the space to carry these extra radios and in particular the auxiliary generator set needed to power them, the ammunition load of the Panther was reduced by 15 rounds in the D and A models and 12 in the G model in the Pz.Bef.Wg to free up space. Although the crew remained the same at five

RIGHT The ceramic holder of the star antenna on the deck of the Münster Tank Museum Panther Ausf A Sd.Kfz. 267 command tank.

FAR RIGHT The turret radio aerial mount as seen on the Münster Tank Museum Panther Ausf A.

men, the loader doubled up as the second radio operator.

It was the extra radio fit of the vehicle – whether it carried a FuG 7 (20W transmitter and VHF receiver) or FuG 8 (30W transmitter and medium-wave receiver) – that determined its designation, and these tanks were pre-wired by MAN on the production lines with the antenna for their use. They could be differentiated by the position of the two/three aerials that either carried. In both cases a GG 400 generator was fitted to the tank to supply the extra electrical power for the additional communications equipment.

The Sd.Kfz. 267 carried an extra FuG 8 radio and had a *Sternantenne D* – better known as a 'star antenna' – mounted within a short cylinder-shaped, porcelain-insulated *Antennenfuss Nr 1*. This was located on the rear of the engine deck.

The Sd.Kfz. 268 could be recognised by the location of its primary antenna for the extra FuG 7 radio it carried. This was 1.4m high and

ABOVE An often-reproduced image of a Panzerbefehlswagen Panther Ausf D, wearing Zimmerit, built just before production switched to the Ausf A in September 1943. It shows the full aerial suite of the Sd.Kfz. 267 variant. It is also fitted out with the 24-bolt road wheels.

was to be found on the left-hand side of the rear hull. The aerial for the FuG 5 was on the turret roof, as for the Sd.Kfz. 267. However, in many cases, those completed as Panzerbefehlswagen Panthers left the factory carrying all three antennae irrespective of the radio fit, so it is not always possible to be certain whether one is looking at a 267 or a 268.

The need for more Panthers fitted out for the command role was such that conversions were undertaken in the field by the *Werkstatt* units. This did not, however, transform such Panthers into fully fledged Panzerbefehlswagen Panthers and the number of examples of these converted was not great.

LEFT The combined FG1250 infrared searchlight and scope attached to the cupola of this Panther. MNH received an order to equip all Panthers they built with this equipment in January 1945.

CENTRE This same infra-red equipment seen from the rear. It is also shown in Chapter 4, page 98, as fitted to the Koblenz Panther Ausf G.

INFRA-RED CAPABILITY ON PANTHERS

Drawing on development experience that went back as far as 1936, a practical (albeit basic) infra-red night-vision device had been created by AEG and had been successfully tested in 1942. It was Guderian who demanded that this facility be made available for use on the Panther to allow the tank to be used at night without fear of attack by enemy aircraft. The specification for the new device was that it had to provide 360-degree vision for the tank commander – even if that meant he had to have his head outside and not under cover. The beam had to be sufficiently powerful to enable the commander to provide directions to the driver via the internal microphone and to enable the gunner to employ his sights to aim at a target. The device was to be attached to a ring on the cupola and this is illustrated both in the images here and seen in Chapter 4 (see page 98), which includes the infra-red equipment on the Panther G at Koblenz.

Maximum range of the sight was just 100m, with the power for the beam deriving from an auxiliary generator carried within the hull and this, in practice, was not very effective. For example, the use of the device left the driver blind. To supplement the infra-red sight on the Panther, a much more powerful infra-red searchlight device was mounted in what had been the troop compartment of an SPW (*Schutzenpanzerwagen*) 251 armoured personnel carrier. Appropriately called the *Uhu* or Owl, this machine would work in tandem with the infra-red-equipped Panthers and 60 of a planned 600 were built. By war's end, some 1,000 of the infra-red sights to be employed on the Panther had been produced. The technology saw very little service but examples of it fell into the hands of both the Allies and the Soviets who developed their own infra-red sights for their main battle tanks post-war based on this technology.

RIGHT To provide an infra-red searchlight of greater power to aid the Panther in night fighting, one was fitted into the troop compartment of the Sd.Kfz. 251. It was designated the Sd.Kfz. 251/20. This variant of the 251 was appropriately called the *Uhu* (Owl).

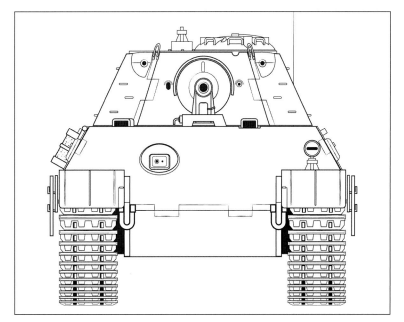

Panther Ausf F

The Ausf F was scheduled to follow on from the Ausf G on the production lines but the war ended before this could begin.

Main changes to the Ausf F:

- The primary change was the installation of the new *Schmalturm*.
- Hull roof plate thickened to 25mm.
- Redesigned driver's/loader's hatches that could be lifted slightly then moved to the side.
- Hull MG 34 replaced by an MG 42.
- Facility to quickly convert panzer to become

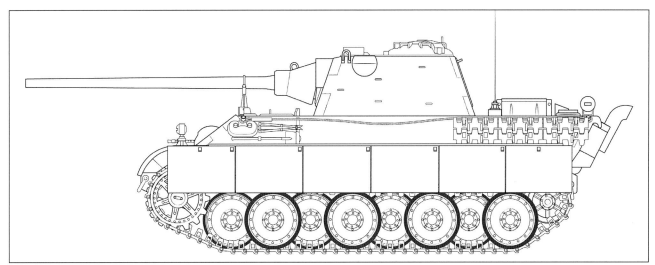

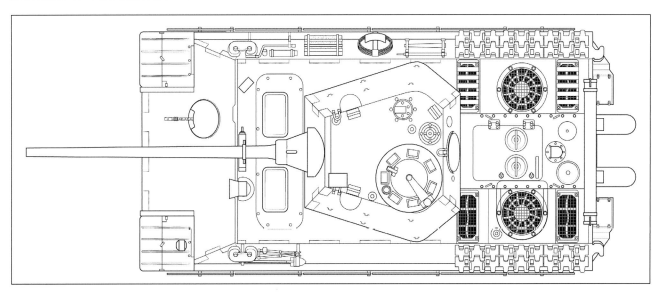

Panzerbefehlswagen Panthers by adding extra radios to the ultra-shortwave radio carried as standard.

■ Extra radios referred to above carried only in the turret.

■ All Ausf Fs to carry two aerial sockets as standard.

■ All Ausf Fs to be equipped so as to be able to employ FG1250 infra-red night-sighting equipment.

■ All production Ausf Fs would have the steel-rimmed 'silent bloc' road wheels, as seen on a number of very later war Ausf Gs.

It is thought that some eight hulls were produced by DB in 1945. Only a few prototype *Schmalturme* had been completed by war's end. DB delivered an Ausf F model chassis in early 1945. It had interleaved all-steel road wheels and mounted an Ausf G turret. (50)

A number of the completed turrets were taken back to the USA and UK.

Panther variants: part three

Only two variants of the Panther other than the tank entered production before the war ended. However, a number of prototypes were made and would have entered production had the war continued.

Bergepanther (Sd.Kfz. 179)

The need for a recovery tank for the Panther was recognised early on. Although not as heavy as the Tiger I heavy panzer, it was accepted that the new medium tank at 45 tons all-up weight posed problems when it came to the recovery of damaged machines. The standard heavy recovery machine prior to the Bergepanther was the Sd.Kfz. 9, an 18-ton half-track. These were used by the *Werkstatt* companies of the tank divisions but were never available in the numbers required. And while the intention was to produce a 35-ton heavy tractor – designated the Sd.Kfz. 20 for this purpose – it was never built. The problem therefore persisted.

Recovery of the Tiger – which went into service before the Panther – indicated that three 18-ton half-track recovery vehicles would be required to effect a retrieval. Although not as heavy as the Tiger, the Panther, at between 44 and 45 tons, would also need such service. These recovery machines could themselves become casualties when their engines became overstressed by the need to recover this new generation of much heavier panzers in the inimical conditions that were experienced on the Eastern Front. Although the use of captured (*Beutepanzer*) KVs and T-34s alongside the Sd.Kfz. 9 half-tracks was sanctioned, this was at best an expedient and not a true solution. To that end it was recognised that a specialist recovery vehicle based on a Panther chassis would be needed to recover an immobilised Panther and, just

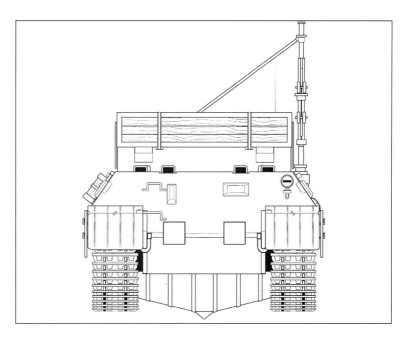

RIGHT AND BELOW Bergepanther Ausf A.
(Mark Rolfe)

three months after the very first Panther left MAN's production line in March 1943, the decision was taken to a create a properly designed Bergepanther – a recovery Panther.

The first 12 built in June 1943 were simply taken from MAN's production line, sans the turret, to function in a recovery role, the hole for the turret being covered with a tarpaulin. As such, the fit of equipment was basic. They lacked proper recovery equipment such as tow bars, beams, winch and rear-fitted spade included on the later production Bergepanthers. Four of these recovery vehicles – designated as *schlepper* – saw service at Kursk, where

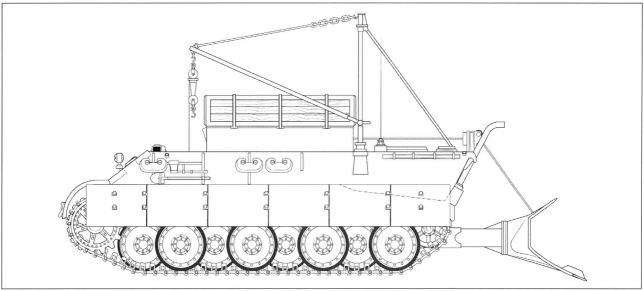

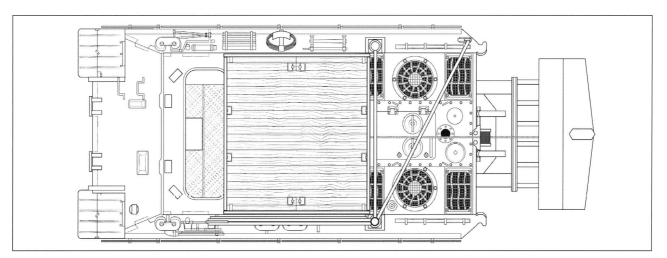

ABOVE While the
Bergepanther was fully
capable of recovering
the Panther, the task
of salvaging the heavy
Tiger not only placed
a strain on its towing
equipment, but it also
stressed its drive-train
components. This is
a late Bergepanther
using the Ausf G
chassis, on display in
France at the Musée
des Blindes in Saumur.
(Wikimedia Commons)

the primary method of recovery was the employment of steel cables, with the two Panther *abteilungen* (battalions) there each fielding four recovery Panthers as well.

The recognition that a properly designed and equipped Bergepanther was needed saw the first leave the production line in June 1943. In total, 232 of these were built utilising the Ausf A chassis. Of these, 70

were constructed by Henschel between July and November 1943 (they ceased production of the Panther in that month). Demag was then ordered to cease building the Panther tank and instead concentrate only on building the Bergepanther from February 1944. These were constructed on the Ausf A chassis until September 1944, then they built another 107 through

RIGHT A very early
Panther hull used as
a basic Bergepanther.
In this case, the crew
have erected some
sort of protection
around the turret
opening.

LEFT Only two
s.Zgkw. 18-ton
Sd.Kfz. 9 half-tracks
were needed on this
occasion to recover a
broken-down Panther
in Russia. This is
due to it being in the
summer where the
ground is hard. But in
the *rasputitsa* – the
rainy season just
before the winter or at
its end – the ground
would be so muddy as
to require three, that
is, of course, if they
were available.

BELOW Difficulty in
extracting bogged-
down or damaged
tanks accounts for the
need for a purpose-
built Bergepanther.
Properly equipped
with a hydraulically
operated spade on the
rear of the hull which,
when dug-in, provided
traction in a recovery
and a powerful winch
mounted in the hull,
this was the machine
that could recover
Panthers.

to March 1945 employing the Ausf G
chassis. A token number of eight were built
employing converted Panther tanks. When
allied troops occupied the factories building
Bergepanthers they were informed that
many of those that had been built actually
used converted and rebuilt Panther tank
chassis.

All of these machines were far better
equipped than the initial tranche. A large
spade was fixed to the rear of the hull, which
was employed for recovery with a 40-ton
capacity winch and a 1.5-ton capacity
derrick. The space in the hull where the
turret basket would have been located was
now taken up by the machinery necessary
to permit those elements to operate. The
Werkstatt company of each Panther unit
was equipped with between two and four
Bergepanthers. For self-protection the
Bergepanther could carry two MG 34s, with
some built on early Ausf A chassis carrying
a 20mm KwK30 fitted to a mount welded
to the glacis. As more battalions converted
to Panthers throughout the latter part of
1943 and into 1944, there was a need for

more recovery vehicles and these machines
became valuable in their own right. They
served in the East, in Italy and in the north-
west of Europe. Many Panthers which were
recovered by these specialist machines would
otherwise have to have been abandoned.

It is worth noting that a number of
these machines were in turn employed as
Munitionspanzers. This was a standard
Bergepanther which had the spade, winch and
derrick withdrawn, in order to permit the space

to be taken up for the carriage and resupply of ammunition.

Jagdpanther (Sd.Kfz. 173) 8.8cm PaK43/3 auf *PanzerJäger* Panther

The concept of a Jagdpanzer was a singularly German concept. Design of a well-armoured and well-protected armoured fighting vehicle (AFV) specifically for the purpose of 'hunting and destroying enemy tanks', although emulated by a number of other nations, found especial favour with the German Army. Its particular design features – the mounting of a high-velocity, powerful gun with limited traverse in an enclosed armoured body – was in contradistinction to the more numerous *PanzerJäger* – which employed essentially the same idea, but placed the gun on an open-topped and lightly armoured and protected body employing the chassis of an obsolescent panzer.

The Germans developed a number of these types, including the Jagdpanzer IV, with initially a 75mm L/48 main weapon, later up-gunned to carry the same 75mm L/70 as the Panther. There was also the extremely heavy 88mm-armed Jagdpanzer Elefant and the later 128mm-armed Jagdpanzer Jagdtiger based on the Tiger II chassis. But it is generally conceded that best of all machines in this class was that based on the chassis of the Panther. Seen as essentially defensive weapons, they could be produced in quite large numbers and at a lower cost than panzers – certainly factors appealing to Hitler in the last two years of the war, as he set great store in such machines. There is, however, little dispute that the most effective of all of Jagdpanzers was that built employing the chassis of the Panzerkampfwagen V Panther and named the Jagdpanther.

88mm Jagdpanzer V: Jagdpanther Number produced: 419 between January 1944 and March 1944	
Fgst.Nr: 300001–300392	
Manufacturer	**Number built**
MIAG (Mühlenbau und Industrie AG)	270
MNH	112
MBA (Maschinenbau und Bahnbedarf)	37

The decision to employ the Panther chassis as the basis of a heavy tank destroyer mounting the 88mm PaK43 L/71 was taken by Wa Prüf 6 in early August 1942, although it required a complete redesign of the tank for it to fulfil that role. Prior to that date it was planned that a heavy tank destroyer mounting the Krupp-designed 88mm PaK44 would utilise the chassis of the Panther II.

Although initially the design product of Krupp, in September 1942 oversight of the project was transferred to DB in Berlin. In the meantime, Krupp had already produced a 1:1 wooden mock-up which was inspected on 16 November 1942. With the abandonment of the Panther II, which had been the original basis for the Jagdpanzer Panther, on 2 October 1942, development switched to the employment of Panther Ausf G as the basis of the design.

An armoured casemate was created by extending the glacis armour and side armour upwards to meet a roof which was tilted forward from the rear at a shallow angle. The angles and thicknesses of the armour to be employed on this new variant of the Panther was as follows:

Armour (mm @ angle) All rolled homogeneous armour	Front	Side	Rear	Top/bottom
Superstructure	80mm @ 55 degrees	50mm @ 30 degrees	40mm @ 35 degrees	25mm @ 83 degrees and 16mm @ 90 degrees
Hull	60mm @ 55 degrees	40mm @ 0 degrees	40mm @ 25 degrees	
Hull bottom				30mm @ 0 degrees
Gun mantlet	100mm – *Saukopfblende*			

The shape of the casemate can be ascertained from a perusal of the three-view drawing of the design shown here.

The first prototype of the Jagdpanzer Panther was first demonstrated at the Arys testing ground in East Prussia on 20 October 1943, and then to Hitler on 16 December 1943 to his evident satisfaction (as he was advocating that the Jagdpanzer be built in greater numbers even than panzers). Production was begun in January 1944 by Mühlenbau und Industrie AG (hereafter MIAG) – a company that had hitherto not been involved in the production of the Panther. MNH joined in production in November 1944, and

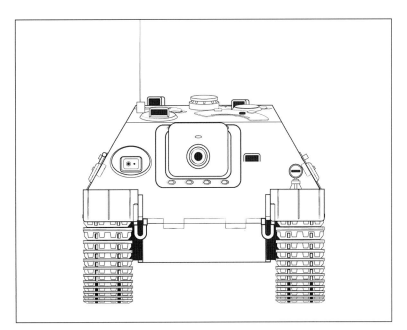

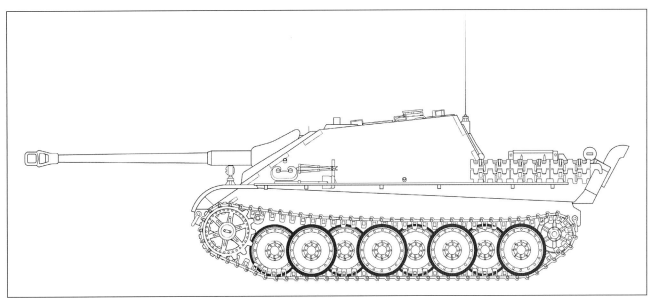

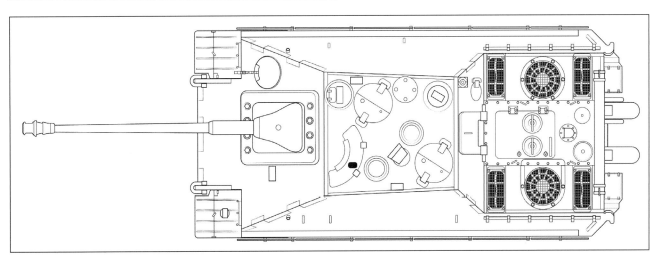

RIGHT The prototype Jagdpanther at the Arys testing ground in East Prussia, in late 1943. It was demonstrated to Hitler a few weeks later.

BELOW s.Pz.Jg. Abt 654 became one of the principal operators of the new Jagdpanther. Its machines and crews are seen undergoing training at Grafenwöhr, Germany, in early 1944.

one month later so did Maschinenbau und Bahnbedarf (MBA). A total of 419 Jagdpanthers were produced by war's end (some sources quote a lower number, for example, Walter Spielberger cites 384). In February 1944, the decision was made to halt production of the Jagdpanther at 450 vehicles – just 37 more than the number actually produced.

The Jagdpanther was equipped with the same HL 230P30 engine as the Panther series, but it was fitted with a new and improved gearbox relative to that on the standard Panther tank. That incorporated by MIAG on the Jagdpanther was a new design manufactured by the firm Zahnradfabrik Friedrichshafen (ZF), and it was the intention

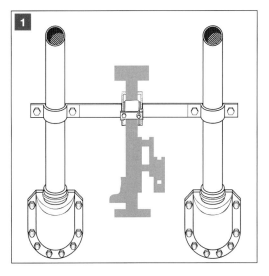

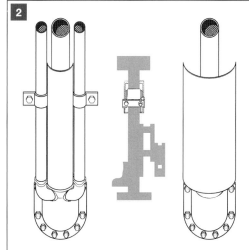

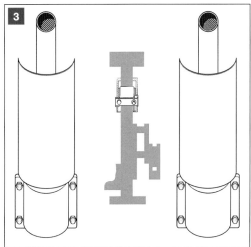

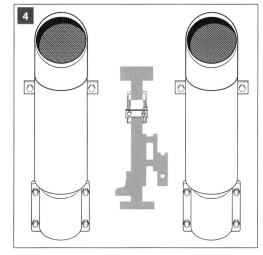

to also incorporate this on Panthers from MAN and DB as part of the OKH improvement programme for the Panther ordered in late 1944, although this did not transpire before the end of the war. The Jagdpanther also suffered the same common problem with the final drive as did the Panther. Most of the Jagdpanthers lost in Normandy were due to mechanical problems, the most common of which was the failure of the final drive, and where possible, these vehicles were blown up by their crews.

The suspension was the same as that employed on the standard Panther Ausf G. The driver was provided with a periscope in the front superstructure to the left of the main gun. The combat weight of the Jagdpanther was very similar to that of the Panther Ausf G at 45.5 tons. A number of Jagdpanthers were also equipped as Panzerbefehlswagen Panthers.

Armament

Apart from the 128mm PaK44 mounted on the Jadgtiger, the 88mm PaK43/3 L/71 (later redesignated PaK43/4) mounted on the Jagdpanther – so renamed on Hitler's order in February 1944 – was the most powerful anti-tank weapon mounted on a Jagdpanzer in the conflict. The weapon had also been mounted earlier on the Ferdinand/Elefant and the Hornisse/Nashorn, which first saw combat in 1943. It was also mounted on the Tiger II heavy tank. It is worth noting that Krupp was involved in investigating the possibility of up-gunning the Jagdpanther to take its 128mm weapon. The weight of the main gun on the Jagdpanther was 1,690kg, inclusive of the barrel, with the breechblock and muzzle brake.

The 88mm PaK43/3 was an immensely powerful weapon such that no Russian or Allied tank could withstand it. When employing Pzgr

ABOVE This formation was relocated to the former French Army tank training ground at Mailly-le-Camp in the late spring of 1944. This particular example is from the early production tranche distinguishable from the latter by its single-piece gun barrel and welded collar surrounding the gun embrasure.

BELOW A later Jagdpanther showing the bolted, removable collar and the two-piece barrel that distinguished it from the early model.

(*Panzergranate*) 40/43 it had a muzzle velocity of 1,130m/sec and could penetrate 153mm of armour at 2,000m. Use of the heavier Pzgr 39-1 shell would see the armour penetration drop off, such that it would penetrate 132mm of armour at the same distance. By 1944, the heaviest frontal armour in enemy tanks was to be found on the Russian JS-II, which had a glacis thickness of 120mm, and the British Churchill Mark VII with 152mm.

The mounting of the main armament within the hull saw it fitted offset from the centreline to the right with the aperture created for the gun in the glacis to project, being quite small. This was surrounded by an armoured collar, initially welded, then later on in the production run bolted on to the glacis, to permit both easy removal of the main gun and also the transmission/gearbox from the hull.

The gun was provided with a limited degree of lateral movement – a total of 22 degrees, that is + or –11 degrees either side of the centreline of the weapon. It thus suffered from the same limitation, irrespective of the power of its main gun, that if outflanked by an enemy, it could only confront them by turning the whole machine on its tracks to fire at them. Although the intention was to try to take out the enemy at distance, if that was not possible and the Jagdpanther could not move in time, then it was certainly vulnerable on its flank in much the same way as the Panther to calibres of weapon that could not penetrate the glacis. Elevation of the main gun went from +14 to –8 degrees. The recoil distance of the main gun within the hull once fired was normally 550mm.

A secondary weapon in the form of an MG 34 was fitted to a ball mount – as on the Panther – to the left of the main gun.

Ammunition totals – 60 main rounds and 600 for the MG 34.

A mounting for a 27mm *Nahverteidigungswaffe* (close defence weapon) was provided for in the roof of the Jagdpanther, although this was not always fitted.

Ammunition

1) *Panzersprenggeschoss* 39 Pzgr39/43
   Cartridge length: 1,124mm
   Ammunition weight: 23.4kg
   Muzzle velocity: 1,000m/sec

RIGHT Mounting the 88mm PaK43 L/71 gun, the Jagdpanther was the most formidable tank destroyer of the war. It served on both the Eastern and Western Fronts.

Penetration at 2,000m: 154mm at 90-degree entry angle

2) *Panzergeschoss mit Stahlkern* 40 Pzgr40/43 W
Cartridge length: 1,124mm
Ammunition weight: 19.9kg
Muzzle velocity: 1,130m/sec
Penetration at 2,000m: 175mm at 90-degree entry angle

3) *Sprenggranate* 43
Cartridge length: 1,170mm
Ammunition weight: 18.7kg
Muzzle velocity: 750m/sec.

Service use

The Jagdpanther was destined for service in the heavy tank destroyer units of the Army which had formerly used the Ferdinand/Elefant. They were employed in small numbers on both the Eastern and Western Fronts, where they saw combat with s.Pz.Jg.Abt 654 (Heavy Tank Destroyer Battalion 654) in Normandy during Operation Bluecoat.

BELOW A fine image that shows the Jagdpanther wearing Zimmerit and the *Schürzen.* Weighing in at 46 tons, it was a little heavier than the standard Panther.

Chapter Three

Anatomy of the Panther

Although the Panther was in production for just 28 months, the design underwent changes in the light of combat experience, with the last variant, the Ausf G, emerging in early 1944 as the most effective. This chapter reviews the generic features of the three Panther tank variants as well as addressing those that are distinctive to each.

OPPOSITE Found directly behind the front drive sprockets was the small rubber-tyred wheel that prevented the tracks from backing up when they were used in reverse. These were replaced by a solid metal skid shoe in the last Ausf Gs produced.

Introduction

What follows in this chapter is a generic coverage of the anatomy of the Panther. Reference to part two will give the more specific characteristics of the three production variants.

Part one: the hull exterior

The design and construction of the Panther hull was the responsibility of the MAN company, with that of the turret and its armament being that of RM. Coverage of details of the turret will be addressed after matters pertaining to the hull have been covered.

The angles of the armour on the Panther drew heavily on those of the Russian T-34 medium tank. These had already been reflected in MAN's cancelled VK 20.02(M) design with the company's VK 30.02 design submission employing these same angles, although the thickness of the armour was greater than that found on the T-34. As we have seen, the order to increase the thickness of the glacis plate was raised from the original 60mm to 80mm at the time MAN received the contract to build the tank. It was, however, Hitler's belief that even 80mm would not be thick enough to protect the Panther in 1943, and it was this that prompted the move towards the creation of the Panther II with 100mm-thick glacis armour. That the Panther II did not translate into a production model saw the original Panther hull kept in production retaining its original 80mm frontal armour through to the end of the war. The table below gives thickness of the various plates used to construct the hull of the Panther and their respective angles. The details of the same for the turret will be addressed in the relevant section on page 87.

The two *Versuchsfahrgestelle* produced by MAN differed from those that later came off the production line in that they were constructed of mild steel and not armour plate. Nor were they constructed of interlocked plates, instead being butt joint welded. The first 20 tanks produced had the 60mm glacis plate as laid down in the original VK 30.02 specification issued by Wa Prüf 6. It was these that were issued to the first two Army units in January 1943.

It was only on the Ausf G that steps were taken to improve the thickness of the superstructure side plate, although the angle slope was reduced from 40 to 30 degrees. As early as Kursk, the 40mm armour on the flanks of the hull had proven particularly susceptible to penetration by the Soviet 7.62cm anti-tank gun.

That this had not been addressed earlier – as with other known problems – was due to the prohibition by Speer in 1943 to reduce time and effort spent on development/ rehabilitative work when this impacted on the output from the production lines. The Panther II had also been intended to redress this matter by virtue of being more heavily armoured, but once the decision had been taken to discontinue this project, the standard Panther was retained in production. Such was the need to get as many Panthers into service, that it was deemed more important to accept them with known problems, even if it was the case that the producers knew what those were – and how to solve them.

Position of plates	Angle of plate Ausf D/A degrees	Angle of plate Ausf G degrees	Thickness of plate Ausf D/A (mm)	Thickness of plate Ausf G (mm)
Glacis plate	55*	55*	80*	80*
Nose plate	55	55	60	50
Superstructure side plate	40	30	40	50
Hull side plate	0	0	40	40
Deck plate	90 horizontal	90 horizontal	16	16
Rear plate	30	30	40	40
Belly plate front/rear	0/0		30/16	

* 80mm of armour set at 55 degrees confers equivalent thickness of 185mm.

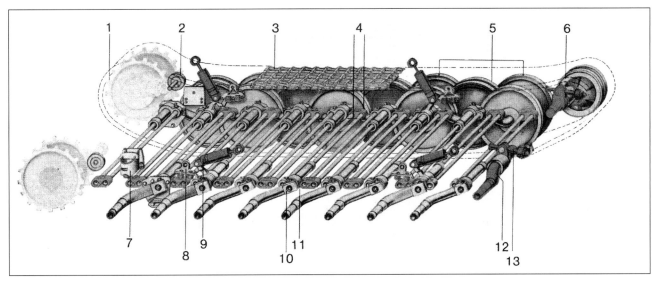

Armour types

Over the course of its production three distinct types of armour were employed on the Panther hull: face-hardened armour (FHA), rolled homogeneous armour (RHA) and cast homogeneous armour (CHA).

FHA was created by a process which took already-created armour plate and then reheated it to further harden what would become the external face of the armour. It was initially employed on the Panther Ausf D on the glacis and all other armoured surfaces including the turret through to August 1943 when it was decided FHA would no longer be used for the glacis, although it was retained on all other forward-facing armoured surfaces as well as on the superstructure sides and rear of the hull.

The replacement of the FHA formed glacis with RHA began in July 1943 and continued through to September 1944 on the Ausf As and Ausf Gs produced from March through to September 1944. In that month all companies producing the Panther were ordered to switch to employing RHA in place of FHA on the turret, hull and superstructure. The particular nature of RHA prevented its use for anything other than the creation of flat armoured plates. These were then cut and welded for use. The primary advantage of RHA lay in its ability to absorb the impact of shock of enemy high-explosive (HE) and armour-piercing (AP) shells.

RHA could not, for example, be used in casting. This accounts for the employment of CHA throughout the production life of the Panther for the curved mantlet of the tank and from August 1943 onward for the tank commander's cast cupola. CHA was also used for the two types of gun collar employed on the Jagdpanther.

Suspension

As we have already seen, it was the particular form of the torsion bar system proposed by MAN for its Panther design that was an influential factor in its selection. It had been designed by Professor Dr Ing Lehr of MAN to allow for the smoothest possible ride across terrain, while not impinging upon performance. It especially permitted the tank to absorb and ride out hard shocks – a factor of great importance for the crew. It also distributed the load of the tank over a larger number of road wheels – hence reducing the ground pressure (see the section on tracks, page 70).

The novel nature of Lehr's design was its employment of a dual torsion bar, in contradistinction to a single torsion bar, which had hitherto been the norm. This permitted a vertical wheel stroke of 500mm – that is, the distance that the wheel could travel up and down – when compared to that of a single torsion bar which had a travel distance of just 220mm. While the dual torsion bar suspension had its detractors, it was nevertheless argued by MAN that from a production point of view it allowed for the best utilisation of resources relative to those others available. As this system was contained within the armoured hull, it was far better protected than other suspension systems that were mounted externally. The Panther hull did, however, require greater initial

ABOVE **A superb colour graphic from a MAN company manual on the Panther showing the workings of the double torsion bar suspension system used on the design.**

1 Drive wheel
2 Support roller
3 Track
4 Torsion bar spring (double)
5 Road wheel
6 Roller wheel
7 Bump stop
8 Yoke
9 Shock absorber
10 Swing arm
11 Connecting rod
12 Idler crank
13 Track tensioner.

RIGHT Clearly seen are the swing arms of the double torsion bar of the Panther as well as the idler wheel on the rear of the hull. This version of the wheel was replaced on the Ausf G.

BELOW Another fine colour graphic illustrating the structure of the swing arm and its links into the hull where it joins up with the double torsion bar which would be fixed to the far side of the hull.

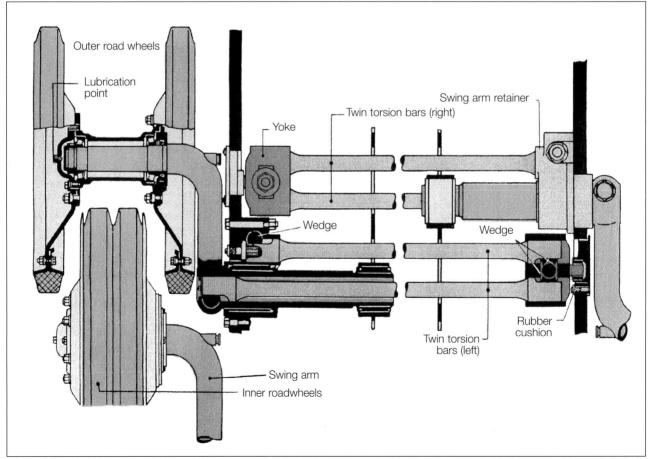

Outer road wheels

Lubrication point

Yoke

Twin torsion bars (right)

Swing arm retainer

Wedge

Wedge

Rubber cushion

Twin torsion bars (left)

Swing arm

Inner roadwheels

preparatory work in terms of the man hours employed in generating the many holes in the hull required to take the suspension arms, which in turn led to higher costs.

As can be seen in the accompanying diagrams and photograph, each of the eight swing arms on either side of the hull were serviced by a dual torsion bar within the hull, which were connected to the road wheels. These were manufactured by Dittman and Neuhaus in the Ruhr area and were designed for a maximum stress of 100,000lb/sq in. It had been stipulated by the OKH that, in the interest of serviceability, the torsion bars be interchangeable right and left. However, problems were initially experienced in the supply chain as the 420mm-long swing arms were of quite complex manufacture, being partially hollow and forged in nature and formed in two parts. The first of these was anchored in the hull and connected to the torsion bar by a yoke. This was welded on to the second section which supported the road wheel. This was initially straight when first manufactured, then bent through 90 degrees to achieve its final shape as the road wheel axle.

On previous panzers, shock absorbers for the suspension were mounted externally, but the employment of large overlapping road wheels on the Panther meant there was no space on the outside of the hull, therefore they had to be mounted within it. The suspension was provided with four shock absorbers mounted on the inside of either side of the hull with one each above the second and seventh

road wheel arms. Each operated independently but only functioned in the vertical plane. They were produced by Hemscheid-Wuppertal, also in the Ruhr area.

In common with all other German tanks from the Panzer I through to the Tiger II, the drive sprockets which conveyed the motive power to the tracks was located at the front of the hull. This power, generated by the motor, was routed through the driveshaft which ran along the base of the hull, above the torsion bars to the transmission (gearbox). Here the motive power was routed through the gears, which had a large gear ratio in order to reduce the transmission speed. Although, as we shall see when we look in more detail at the transmission, that fitted to the Panther was designed for its lighter progenitor, which was to bring problems of reliability in its train. However, it was noted for providing increased torque to the drive sprocket but that in turn put stress on the final drive – the weakest aspect of the Panther design.

The idler wheel at the rear of the hull was adjustable. This was located on a cranked axle that rested within the hull. The same type of idler wheel was used throughout the production of the first tank models, being only changed with the onset of the Ausf G. The new and larger idler wheel was fitted by all manufacturers except for DB, who continued to fit the original

BELOW The same idler wheel was carried by the Ausfs D and A but was replaced with a new design on the Ausf G. The latter was self-cleaning, so did not get clogged up with snow or mud.

wheel. The new, larger idler wheel was self-cleaning, thus preventing the build-up and solidifying of mud and snow – as happened often in the East.

Such was the effectiveness of the suspension that it was noted that the chassis was always stable when the main gun was fired, but the Panther was unable to fire on the move.

Road wheels

The Panther was equipped with eight pairs of dished road wheels per side – each being of 860mm diameter – and were manufactured by Kronprinz of Solingen. Moving rearwards from the front, the first, third, fifth and seventh of the pairs of road wheels were double. These were overlapped on the inside and outside on the other road wheel stations by single wheels. The inner road wheels mounted the track guide rings. There was a guide roller attached to the housing of the final drive. This was, however, replaced on very late production Ausf Gs by a solid metal *Gleitschuh* (skid shoe). This can be seen on the Tank Museum Panther in Chapter 4 (see page 110).

The road wheels were interleaved and

mounted rubber tyres. As the rubber of the tyres had not been hardened by vulcanisation, they could be removed in the field by the use of a sledgehammer and replaced with new ones. It was the tyres, however, that provided tank crews with one of the most common problems afflicting the Panther throughout its production life. The problem arose from the failure of the rim bolts holding the rubber tyre to the road wheel. A total of 18 rim bolts were employed on each road wheel of the *Versuchsfahrgestelle*, this number being reduced on the production models to 16 per road wheel. This was not a sensible decision in that the smaller number accentuated the stress generated on the road wheels that led to the failure of the rim bolts. Fitting of 16 rim bolts continued as standard on the Ausf D, only being changed during the course of the production of the Panther Ausf A, when stronger road wheels with 24 rim bolts were introduced in August 1943. However, Panther As were seen with road wheels with both types as old stock of the 16 rim bolt wheels were used up even as the 24 rim bolt wheel began to be fitted. The 24 rim

bolt wheel was retained on the Ausf G and on the Jagdpanther. It would seem, however, that even this did not solve the problem, with the distances at which they failed ranging from 0 to 5,000km. The latter figure was very rarely ever achieved, with few road wheels known to go to the design maximum. This ongoing problem for tank crews frequently accounts for those images wherein one or two spare road wheels and even spare tyres are shown mounted on a Panther.

Although the suspension of the Panther gave the crew a good ride when functioning properly, should the need arise to replace a road wheel or a tyre on a road wheel, then the process of

ABOVE **Although the particular suspension type of the Panther made for a smooth ride, in practice replacement of a tyre on one of the inner road wheels entailed the chore of having to prise off the outer ones first.**

LEFT **One example of the many photographs taken by the Germans which shows a Panther carrying spare road wheels. The continuing problem with their failure was never solved and these panzers could be seen carrying them through to the end of the conflict.**

wheel removal required much effort and was extremely time consuming. Problems with the wheel axles or the torsion bars necessitated the road wheels being removed so that the respective problems could be addressed.

Tracks

It was understood at the time the Panther was being designed by MAN (and indeed DB) that track width was a significant concern. The T-34 had demonstrated an ability to move across terrain that was difficult for the Panzers III and IV, especially so in the period known as the *rasputitsa* – the mud season or 'time without roads', which preceded the winter and of course, the snow in the East. Whereas the two German tanks had tracks with a width of approximately 40cm, the T-34 tracks were 51cm wide. This resulted in the T-34, though heavier than either German tank, having a lower ground pressure, which permitted it to go where the two Panzer types could not. The Marks III and IV frequently grounded in mud and snow whereas the T-34 was able to traverse both conditions fairly easily.

Even after the glacis of the Panther was raised to 80mm, with a corresponding increase of the tank to 44 tons, the track was not enlarged to take account of the increase in weight. A figure of 12.089lb/sq in still permitted the Panther an effective ground pressure that remained superior to that of the T-34 and indeed the US M4, an advantage shared with the Tiger heavy tank that weighed 12 tons more than the Panther. This may seem strange given how much heavier the two German tanks were, but both shared a similar type of suspension of overlapping road wheels that distributed the weight of the tank over a larger number of road wheels. Once in service both tanks were able to traverse terrain difficult for the Panzers III, IV and assault guns. It was generally acknowledged by both the British and US Armies that the Panther was more manoeuvrable than any Allied tank.

A total of 86 individual links formed each track on the Panther. Spare track links were often carried on the hull and, although frowned upon, they were also carried on the turret where most were perceived as functioning as 'extra' armour.

BELOW The Panther was better able than its normal stablemate the Panzer IV to cope with the appalling muddy conditions experienced in Russia at certain times of the year. Its wider track reduced the ground pressure of the machine, enabling it to cope, whereas the Mark IV would become grounded in the morass.

Composed of steel, the links were held together by steel pins that did not have any bushings, which resulted in the track being fairly easy to repair. Each track was cast and had an inbuilt facility for the attachment of a snow grouser, which permitted the tank to achieve a stronger grip in deep snow. However, conditions in Russia could become so bad – especially in the thaw – that even Panthers sank in the mire and 'grounded'. Russian photographs taken in early 1944, when the thaw came unusually early in the southern theatre, shows Panthers abandoned by their crews because they could not be extricated in time from the very deep mud.

A document from 1944 circulated to German tank commanders drew attention to a number of problems incurred when operating the Panther. Two specific observations were made concerning the tracks:

Tracks and track adjustment: the Panther track is correctly adjusted when the track just touches the second bogie wheel from the front, i.e. when further tensioning would lift it off this bogie wheel. Consequently,

when the final stage of the track tensioning process becomes a heavy job, negligent drivers often allow the track to remain too loose. Adjusting collars and retaining pins fall off, so it is essential that the driver should inspect the tracks frequently.

The tracks were adjusted by means of the eccentrically mounted idler wheels. Each idler is moved forward or backwards by means of a worm drive to the swinging arm of the idler.

The same document details a consequence of the build-up of mud or snow in that:

the track of the Panther sometimes slips from the teeth of the driving sprocket and jams, owing to the assemblage of undesirable matter. The consequent tensioning of the track is so great that it is generally not possible to knock out a track pin.

The example given to solve the problem (it happened on the Tiger) was of a crew that blew the links apart with a hand grenade. A very extreme solution – not at all recommended!

BELOW The crewman ponders the track which needs to be rejoined. One of the more straightforward aspects of the Panther was the track – classified as a 'dead track' – in that the links were connected with steel pins with bushings. Note also on the rear hull of the Panther is a spare road wheel.

Panther Ausf A.

(Mark Rolfe)

1 Muzzle brake
2 7.5cm KwK42 L/70 gun
3 Glacis plate, 80mm armour
4 Radio operator's seat
5 Radio operator's hatch
6 Vision blocks
7 Gun mantlet, 100mm curved
  armour
8 Debris guard
9 Turret lifting rings
10 Turret roof, armour 16mm
11 Vision blocks
12 Commander's drum-type
   cupola and hatch
13 Cooling air inlet grilles
14 Stowage bins
15 Twin exhaust pipes
16 Cooling fan
17 Spare track links
18 Turret side armour,
   45mm
19 Gun cleaning tube
20 Commander's seat
21 Gunner's seat
22 Solid rubber tyre
23 Towing shackle
24 Shovel
25 Schürzen
26 Road wheel
27 Single Bosch headlight
28 Drive wheel
29 Driver's seat
30 Steel tracks
31 Towing eyes
32 Driver's hatch
33 Steering box
34 Ball-mounted MG34
   machine-gun
35 Driver's instrument panel
36 Mudguards

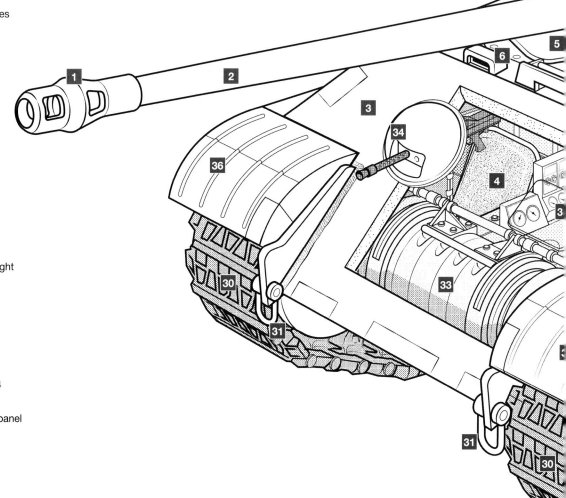

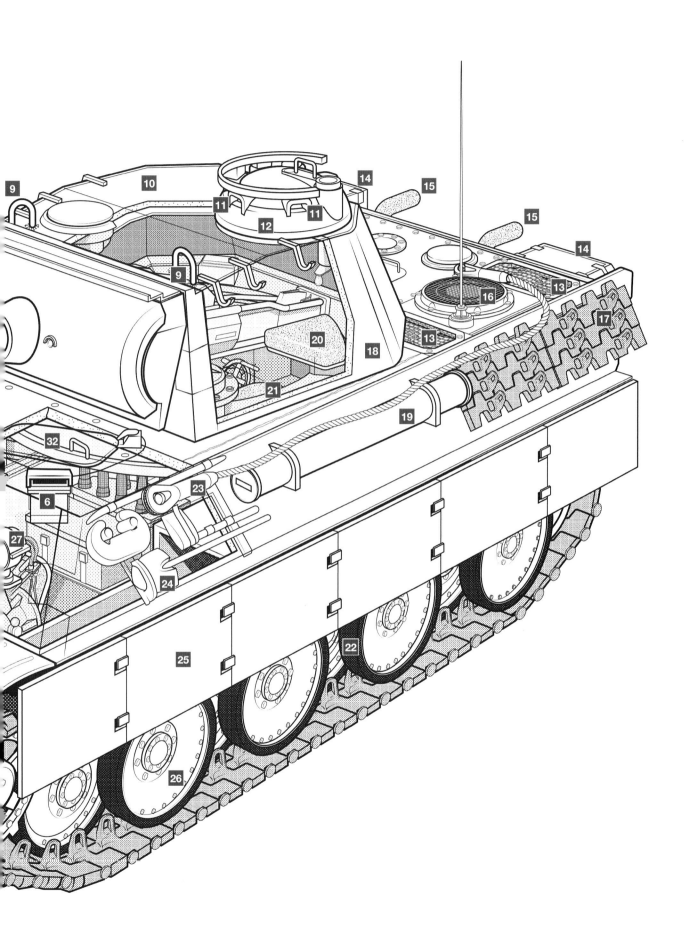

Part two: the hull interior

The hull interior was divided into two sections – namely the crew compartment to the fore, which housed the turret basket, and the engine compartment to the rear, which was separated from the former by a firewall. It is the latter we will consider first.

Part A: the motor

The two *Versuchsfahrgestelle* and the first 20 pre-production Panthers that came off MAN's production line very early in 1943 were fitted with the HL (*Hochleistungs Motor* – high-performance motor) 210 engine as per the original VK 30.02 specification and built by Maybach Motorenwerke. Developing 650hp during testing by MAN and by the Army at Kummersdorf, the first two machines demonstrated that once the thicker 80mm armoured glacis was fitted, the Panther would be underpowered given the growth in its weight. The decision was then taken to equip production machines, after the first 250 built, with the more powerful HL 230 engine.

The 23,000cc HL 230P30 developed 50hp more than the earlier HL 210, conferring on the Panther a power-to-weight ratio of 15.5hp to the ton. It was a liquid-cooled, 12-cylinder, V-type, four-stroke petrol combustion engine with interchangeable lubricated cylinder sleeves. Even though the HL 230 was more powerful than the HL 120 TRM employed in both the Panzer III and Panzer IV – 23,000cc for the former versus 11,687cc for the latter – it was of a very compact size and relatively low weight. This in turn resulted in a reduced size for the engine compartment within the Panther hull, it constituting just 63.7% of the interior space and also contributed to keeping down the weight of the tank and also its overall height.

In common with other German tank engines, the HL 230 engine was equipped with a dry sump lubrication system, with the 25-litre capacity tank mounted on the right of the engine feeding the oil through a pressure pump, an oil cooler and oil filter to the necessary lubricating points. It was stressed to the crew that the oil level should not be permitted to drop below the lower level on the dipstick and must

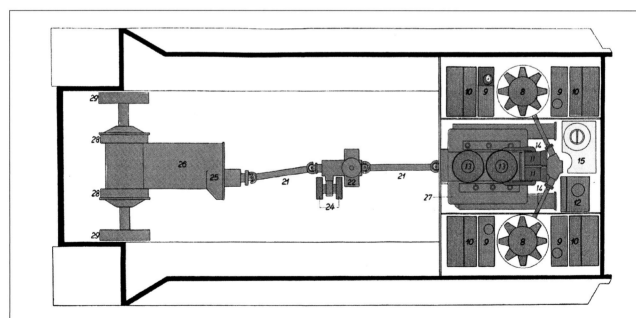

6 Oil cooler for change and unicycle steering gear	**11** Magnet	**15** Fuel keepers	**26** Gearbox (transmission)
	12 Cool water tank	**21** Engine prop shafts	**27** Engine
8 Fan	**13** Air filter	**22** Turret turning motor	**28** Steering gearbox
9 Cooler	**14** Air-fan propulsion	**24** Oil pressure system	**29** Steering brakes.
10 Air guider	shafts	**25** Main clutch	

LEFT The Maybach HL 230P30 V-12 engine was the standard engine for the Panther throughout its entire production run (although the first 250 were built with the HL 210P30).

not be filled above the upper level; this required them to monitor the oil level on a regular basis. A rough check would normally be made at the end of a journey or during a halt on the march; however, it could only take place when the engine was idling at about 800rpm. Thereafter, with the engine turned off and the oil allowed to cool down, a more accurate check could be made followed by a refilling of the oil if required.

There were also quite specific instructions as to when an oil change was required. In all cases it had to take place when the engine was warm. For a new Panther where the engine was being run in, the first change would come after just 250km. Thereafter the frequency would be determined by the conditions the Panther was operating in. In Italy or in a Russian summer, particularly in the south of the country where both heat and dust were problematic, an oil change would be needed every 1,000km.

Under other circumstances, such as in Western Europe, one would be necessary every 2,000km. The oil filter also required careful monitoring with cleaning needed every 1,000km. In the case of changing the engine oil and cleaning the oil filter, there were quite specific steps for the tank crew to follow.

Early operations with the HL 230P30 revealed shortcomings such that in September 1943, Wa Prüf 6 ordered that all the engines that had been delivered were to be replaced with new ones in which the problems had been addressed. This did not, however, cure the fundamental problem that the engine had a limited lifespan in terms of usage. Over-revving the engine also served to reduce its longevity and in yet another attempt to minimise the problem of the short life of the motor the decision was taken to de-rate the HL 230 – reducing the engine to 2,500rpm when at maximum load (with full ammunition plus all fuel, etc). This had the effect of lowering the engine output from the standard 700hp to some 580hp with a corresponding reduction in performance. This saw the top speed fall from 52km/h (34mph) to 45km/h (28mph).

Nonetheless, relative to the summer of 1943, engine performance and reliability had improved but it was far from reaching the degree of effectiveness that would have permitted the Panther to have become what could be called a reliable combat machine. When it worked, it worked well, but far too often many of them did not. Nonetheless, by the early spring of 1944 one battalion commander from Panzer Regiment 1 wrote a report in which he stated:

In general the newer motors have a significantly longer lifespan than the first series. The longest distance achieved by a motor is 1,700 to 1,800km in 3 of the 7 Panthers that are still available. The motor failures that did occur were all of the same nature; bearing damage and broken connecting rods.

The problem with engine fires had not been totally eliminated and they continued to occur.

The same report contained the following observations:

Motor fires also significantly decreased. The proven cases of motor fires at present are:
1) *Oil leaks for the valve covers due to poor gaskets. The oil drops on the hot exhaust where it ignites.*
2) *In several cases, a heavy overflowing coming from the carburettors was noticed. The spark plugs became wet and didn't fire. The unburnt fuel was then discharged to the exhaust header and leaked through the gaskets. This caused fire to spread on the outside of the motor.*

Referring once again to the captured document issued by the British Army to units in Normandy concerning the Panther, it was noted that German observations about the engine stated: '. . . In spite of the improved engine performance – the battalion of Panthers averaged 450 miles per tank with only 11 engines having to be changed.'

In what was a very telling instruction, it was recommended that: 'Panthers *should not be driven over stretches greater than 62 miles* [my italics] as this causes much harm to the suspension [especially in winter].'

It was this similar limitation on distance that applied also to the Tiger I and Tiger II, hence the German Army's employment of the railway system to move Panther units around the various fronts it fought on whenever possible. And this included even short distances – as little as 25km in some cases. Although there is of course evidence for Panthers covering greater distances under their own steam, it must be noted that this was a consequence of circumstances and was thus unusual. That was hardly conceivable when in reality the short fatigue life of the engine lay between just six and seven times the range of the machine.

The Panther's forte was on the immediate battlefield. It could not have achieved the sorts of rates of advance or distance covered by Panzers III and IV in 1940 in the French Campaign, nor the advances into Russia in the summers of 1941 and 1942. Neither could the Panther have emulated the rapid advance of Allied armour across France and Belgium following the end of the Normandy Campaign in 1944, executed by the often-derided M4 and Cromwell tanks.

Cooling system

The cooling system of the Panther comprises two radiator assemblies, each located in its own sealed bulkhead and separated from the engine. The other components that make up the cooling system are as follows:

- A fan for each radiator. These were each driven by a two-speed gear, a two-plate dry clutch, a bevel gear and a driveshaft from the engine.
- The header tank was situated in the engine compartment and had a filler plug.
- The oil cooler for the engine.
- A water pump.
- Connections and valve for the cooling water. Also used for the transfer of cooling water and for the heating apparatus.

The header tank for the radiators is situated in the engine compartment and carries a filler plug which is fitted with a pressure/vacuum valve. This enables the water temperature to reach a temperature of about 105°C without boiling. The water pump itself is driven by a shaft from the governor and is sealed with rubber washers.

The cooling fans are each driven by a two-speed gear, a two-plate dry clutch, a bevel gear and a driveshaft from the engine. To protect the fan driveshafts from overloading due to a sudden acceleration of the motor, each fan is connected to its shaft by a shifting clutch. The bearings and bevel gear that govern the operation of the fans are located below them and are lubricated with engine oil. This must be checked whenever maintenance on the Panther is carried out with the oil itself being changed every 5,000km (however, when an engine is being run in, this is initially 1,000km and thereafter 5,000km). As the oil itself can only be changed when the radiator unit is dismantled for maintenance, it is advised that the opportunity be taken whenever that occurs, even if less than 5,000km since the last change.

The cooling air pipe for cooling the exhaust and the hot air extracted from the engine were directed into the fan compartment. From October 1944 onward, the hot air from the engine directed into the engine compartment was then redirected into the crew compartment. This was realised by forcing the hot air into the fighting compartment by the radiator fans through pipes at the side. For this, the exhaust grille had to be partially uncovered. In order to adapt the cooling to the temperature outside, adjustable fan shutters were incorporated in the fighting compartment.

Fuel system

The Panther was equipped with five built-in fuel tanks holding about 750 litres of petrol. If the fuel tap was set to *Hauptbehälter* (main tank) then about 600 litres was available. The other 150 litres constituted the fuel reserve and could be accessed by switching over to the *Hilfsbehälter* (auxiliary tank). The content of the reserve tank was sufficient for a road journey of between 30 and 40km. Refuelling the Panther required a degree of care as the filler pipe was near the exhaust pipes. These became extremely hot when operating and, even when the engine was stopped, they still took time to cool, therefore a lack of accuracy in refuelling could lead to petrol sloshing on to the exhaust, risking a fire. In addition, the breather holes in the fuel pipe had to be kept open and clean otherwise the fuel delivery would be faulty.

Early on in the Panther's career the fuel pumps caused problems. At Kursk, at least 20 Panthers suffered mechanical failure within three days of the opening of the offensive due to fuel pump leaks. The fuel collected on the floor pan of the engine compartment which then led to fire. At least three were written off for this reason – including two that burst into flames when being unloaded on arrival from Germany.

Such was the potential danger of the refuelling process that the Panther *Fibel* – a specially produced handbook on the tank – was circulated. Directed primarily at younger enlisted men (and by 1944 these were indeed getting younger; many of the older, experienced crewmen having already been killed or wounded in combat – a problem facing all combat arms of the Wehrmacht by that date) the advice and instruction was tempered by the addition of cartoons and risqué images. Here is the advice on refuelling. It does not mince words:

It is clear that the Panther burns quickly when knucklehead Paul sleeps during refuelling! Don't spill any fuel if you want to live longer. Take caution as you go to work! The fuel is mixed with lead, it damages eyes, skin and wounds.

Refuelling by yourself is an art! First check that your canister [Jerrycan] contains gasoline and not diesel. ... Then first clean the funnel. Cap off, leave the sieve in. Always pour fuel carefully when the exhaust pipe is hot! If it is windy, stand with your back to the wind. In rainy or snowy conditions, bend over the fuel tank filling hole to protect it. However, even careful refuelling is useless with leaky fuel lines, connectors and fuel pumps, so double-check all of these! Clean out fuel and dirt that accumulates outside the fuel tanks. Never start the engine if there is oil or fuel in the hull.

The fuel was supplied to the carburettor by two mechanical pumps. Each pump consisted of two diaphragm pumps united by a common plunger drive in the pump housing. Each of the two pumps drew fuel from a common fuel pipe through a suction valve into a common pressure pipe. A fuel filter with an inspection glass is fitted in front of the pump. The crew

were advised to be careful of the washers when cleaning the fuel filter and the inspection glasses had to be cleaned every 500km.

Transmission (gearbox)

The transmission fitted to the Panther was manufactured by Zahnradfabrik Friedrichshafen (ZF) and was selected because it was thought that being of a simpler construction to the alternative chosen for the Tiger I heavy tank, it would prove to be more reliable in service. However, the selection of this gearbox was to bring problems in its train in that it had been selected when the VK 30.02 was envisaged as weighing just 35 tons. At that weight, the ZF transmission would have, in all probability, worked most effectively, but by the time the Panther came into production, its weight had increased by some 9 tons. This was to place a strain on the gearbox which was to lead to it becoming a source of problems in the field. Indeed, a post-war (1946) British Army analysis of the Panther transmission noted that: 'It is likely that the gear ratios were based on the original design weight of some 35 tons, and when the weight of the machine increased to 44 tons some adjustment should have been made to the final drive ratio.'

The ZF transmission employed a synchromesh mechanism for the seven forward gears and one reverse gear. The biggest problems occurred when the driver was effecting a change from second to third speed. The same British Army document noted that: '. . . theoretical analysis shows that a synchronous 2–3 change is improbable and this is confirmed by the statements of prisoners-of-war, and by the damaged condition of the 3rd speed dogs on all the gearboxes examined'.

Such was also confirmed by the captured German document referred to earlier wherein it was noted that:

. . . the third gear of the Panther gearbox is the one most often in use. When changing gear it should therefore be nurtured carefully. In five out of seven cases the gearbox had to be changed because the third gear could no longer be engaged. As the cog wheels of the third gear are always in constant mesh, it becomes impossible to engage a higher gear.

In truth, driving the Panther required more skill from its driver than, say, his US or British counterpart operating an M4. Such is clearly understood by the following observation:

When travelling in second gear, and it is desired to change up to third gear, the vehicle should be accelerated so that during the process of changing gear (particularly over bad ground or a steep incline) it does not come to a halt. If insufficient time for changing gear has been allowed, i.e. if the tank does slow up, the driver should not make the mistake of trying to make up this

ABOVE, LEFT AND BELOW The seven-speed transmission AK 7-200 was designed by Zahnradfabrik Freidrichshafen and in theory could help the Panther realise a top speed of 54km/h. The driver's gear-change handle can be seen on the side of the transmission box. The two colour images show the inner workings of the Panther transmission of a rebuilt example that is on show next to the Bovington Tank Museum's own Ausf G.

time shortage by changing gear quickly. Changing gear too quickly overstrains both the teeth on the cogs and the synchromesh apparatus and incidentally overloads the main drive. When the going is heavy or when a steep hill has to be negotiated, it is therefore preferable to remain in third gear.

It is pertinent to speculate as to just how many Panthers were rendered *hors de combat* by drivers doing exactly what the above observation states they should not do. Hence the need for the repetition of the observation in the document – with this being made in the summer of 1944. It is hardly surprising that the transmission had a poor reputation for reliability and it would seem that where a Panther did manage to proceed without problems coming from the transmission it had much to do with the skill of the driver and his ability to handle the idiosyncrasies of the ZF design. Nonetheless, when the transmission failed and needed to be replaced, it required a crane to lift it from the hull. From June 1944, the need for such was obviated when the welding of three sockets to the roof of the Panther permitted the crew to use a *Behelfskran* – a small jib crane with a 2-ton capacity – to do the same job. Whatever the means employed to facilitate this, the hatch which covered both the driver and radio operator was removed. The transmission could then be detached from the engine driveshaft and lifted out of the Panther's hull. It took the better part of a day for a *Werkstatt* team to replace a transmission.

In a final observation concerning the transmission, we will return to the 1946 British Army document. What could appear as a criticism is rather more reflective of a difference in the British and German approach to gearing provision in their respective tanks: 'On the score of efficiency, the gearbox and steering system should not compare unfavourably with current British AFV transmissions. There are more gears involved in 1st and 2nd speeds than in our designs but this is relatively unimportant.'

It was also the considered judgement of the British evaluation team that the gearbox of the Panther was over-geared and cited gears six and seven as being of little value in helping the Panther in crossing terrain. It did, however,

acknowledge that the provision of these gears was for road use only and that 'in this respect the vehicle is comparable with other German AFVs', while adding the rider that 'where one has a gearbox giving six or more speeds, the luxury of a gear for road use can only be enjoyed'. Clearly one that the British author of the report would have appreciated had he had this in his own tank!

Steering system and brakes

There was some debate as to what type of steering system to employ on the Panther at the beginning of its production life. That finally agreed was an *Einradienlenkgetriebe* (a fixed radius steering gear). This meant that the radius of the curve the driver wished to traverse determined his selection of the gear that permitted him to do so. As there were seven forward gears, he had just seven fixed-radius turn possibilities and they are listed below:

- First gear – provided a fixed turning radius of 16ft or 5m.
- Second gear – provided a fixed turning radius of 36ft or 11m.
- Third gear – provided a fixed turning radius of 59ft or 18m.
- Fourth gear – provided a fixed turning radius of 98ft or 30m.
- Fifth gear – provided a fixed turning radius of 150ft or 46m.
- Sixth gear – provided a fixed turning radius of 200ft or 61m.
- Seventh gear – provided a fixed turning radius of 265ft or 81m.

But not all possible or desirable turns the driver of the Panther might need to make could be reduced to the use of one or other of these fixed-turning radius gears. What did he do if he needed to make one that did not require any of those? He would be forced to have recourse to skid-steer his machine. This involved slowing down one of the two tracks – the one chosen being determined by which direction he wished to turn – and using the Panther's disc brakes. The panzer would then turn in the direction of the slower track. However, a US Army report on the Panther dated 12 January 1945 noted that:

The skid-turn feature of the steering system . . . cannot be employed at speeds in excess of approximately 8 to 10mph [13 to 16km/h], and can only be used when the vehicle is in second gear, as the engine will be stalled if such a turn is made in a higher gear.

It was no doubt for this reason that drivers were instructed to try to avoid having to do this if possible, also because it incurred heavy wear on the track brakes. These were located on the forward lower section of the hull to the left of the driver's foot and to the right of the radio operator's foot. They were enclosed by two ridged covers. Drivers were both warned about and encouraged to employ the radius turns of the gears as much as possible. The brakes were not to be used if a high gear was engaged. In reverse, steering was reversed when using the geared turns. Drivers were told to try to avoid certain situations: for example, steering on a slope should be avoided wherever possible. Rather, the driver should try to ensure that he drove vertically up a slope and begin to steer only when he regained the horizontal. In the same fashion, when going up or down a hill, the driver was told to employ either the handbrake *or* the footbrake. To do otherwise was to risk damage to the transmission. However, given the exigencies of combat it was not always possible to observe these limitations and it was inevitable that the driver would find himself having to do that which he knew he had been trained not to. It is worth noting that in the British Army's assessment of the Panther's transmission and steering, the radii of the turns was thought to be too large.

Final drive
It was, however, the final drive that was the weakest point of the Panther design. That fitted to the production Panther had been designed for the lower-powered HL 210 engine and its

RIGHT The large hatch above the driver's and radio operator's stations was removable to permit field workshop crew to do what they are doing here – that is, removing the transmission from a Panther Ausf G which is in need of replacement or repair.

accompanying ZF-7 gearbox, which was the root of the problem. The additional power of the HL 230, as well as the added weight of the production Panther, overstressed the final drive. So poor was this aspect of the tank that it was deemed to be one of the few parts of the Panther that did not meet its planned fatigue life, with the actual figure being just 150km. Such was the vulnerability of this mechanism that many breakdowns and Panthers in need of repair stemmed from the failure of this element. This is reflected in another section of the earlier-cited report by the battalion commander of Pz.Rgt 1, which serves to illustrate just how many Panthers were affected by this problem:

A very large percentage of Panthers broke down through damage to the final drives. As an example, since the first of March (1944), 13 final drives were replaced in 30 Panthers. More on the left than on the right. Bolts on the large gear inside the final drive shear off. Final drives cannot hold up to steering in reverse on heavy soil.

Indeed, some measure of how common this problem was can be gauged by the fact that after-battle assessment of abandoned Panthers in Normandy by Allied surveyors indicated that at least half of the total number inspected had suffered this problem. Guderian, in his report to Hitler of 28 June 1944, detailing the performance of the *Panzerwaffe* in Normandy, cited the problem with the Panther's final drive and stipulated that 'a solution to the final drive problem is urgently needed'. It certainly was, but this problem had not been solved by the end of the conflict.

Indeed, post-war, the French Army employed 50-plus Panthers and some Jagdpanthers for some years – for a period of time longer than the German Army used the machine – prior to the arrival of US-supplied tanks. In the course of their being operated, certain conclusions about the machine were published in a document called *Le Panther 1947*. The French experience with the problematic final drive led to the following guidelines as to how best to operate the

Panther to avoid too much unnecessary strain on the final drive:

In order to prevent these breaks it is recommended that the following points be closely observed: when driving downhill and in reverse, as well as on uneven terrain, to be particularly careful when shifting to a lower gear. In addition a Panther should never be towed without uncoupling the final drive previously. Finally, under no circumstances should both steering levers be operated simultaneously – regardless of the situation.

However, what is possible in peacetime, where the Panther driver could be trained to treat his charge with a certain degree of delicacy when operating it, was not always possible for German Army Panther drivers given the contingencies that governed combat operations between 1943 and 1945. In the same fashion that Panther crews were instructed (as with those driving the Tiger I) never to employ their own tanks to recover a broken-down colleague, there is enough photographic evidence to show that this injunction was often ignored. It is hardly surprising that given the

known weakness of the final drive, that this was also compounded by its use with the Panther's transmission, in that it too failed for the same reason – the greater power of the HL 230 motor.

Given the short amount of time the Panther was in production and the intense need to get as many to the fronts on which the German Army was fighting – and this is being repeated because it is cited elsewhere – it was accepted for service 'warts and all'. This included living with the known limitation of its final drive.

Part B: the crew compartment

The Panther was designed for a crew of five – the standard crew size for a German medium tank. The driver and radio operator/machine gunner were in the forward section of the hull and the other three in the turret. Although the interior of the Panther could in no way be described as spacious, it was certainly more roomy than either the Panzer III or IV. Whereas MAN was responsible for the hull and RM the turret and armament, it was the OKH that had designed the stowage arrangements and had provided this information to MAN for incorporation into the production machines.

LEFT One of the great bugbears of the life of *Werkstatt* crews was the frequent need to replace the final drives on the Panther. This was the real Achilles heel of the machine, having been originally designed for a lower-weight Panther.

The following steps and procedures (taken from a British document) are those that the driver of a Panther would need to learn in order to start the tank. They had to be observed every time the Panther was started.

Before starting the engine it would be necessary to check the levels of 1) the engine oil, 2) the petrol and 3) the engine water.

1) Oil capacity for the engine was 9 gallons. The oil filler cap is located on right-hand side of engine. Dipstick read 'full'/'low'.

2) The petrol level is checked by unscrewing the header filler tank cap. This is located at the rear of the engine compartment on the right-hand side, beneath a circular armoured cover plate on the engine top plate. Petrol level should be up to the lower edge of the filler. The capacity is approximately 170 gallons.

3) The water level is checked by unscrewing the cap of the header tank filler. This is located at the rear of the engine compartment on the left-hand side beneath a circular armoured cover plate on the engine top plates. This cover plate is the large one. The water level should be up to the lower edge of the filler. Water capacity is approximately 33 gallons.

Make certain that:

a) The gear lever is in neutral.

b) The steering levers are pushed right forward.

c) The handbrake is on – that is, pulled back up the toothed rack.

Starting the engine within the hull

1) Turn on the master switch.

2) Switch on the petrol main tank (*hauptbehälter*) and prime the engine with a few strokes of the primer control.

3) Switch on the ignition key.

4) Press the starter button.

In the event of the electric starter failing to operate, an alternative inertia starter is fitted. Both starters are located at the rear of the engine on the right-hand side. The inertia starter is operated as follows:

a) Unscrew the second armoured plate from the right in the hull rear plate.

b) Into the end of the starter shaft, now revealed, insert cranked starting handle.

c) Crank the starter handle as fast as possible (the 'whirr' of the inertia starter mechanism will be plainly heard).

d) When maximum cranking speed is obtained, pull the looped handle on the end of the chain protruding above the starter shaft sharply outwards. This engages the starter pinion and will turn the engine over sufficiently to start it.

Before driving off

1) Check engine oil pressure. The oil pressure gauge should show approximately 75kg/sq cm.

2) Check the charging rate. The ammeter should show approximately 50 amperes.

Moving off

1) Changing gear. The positions of the lever for obtaining the seven forward and one reverse gear are shown below.

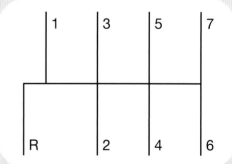

The gears are selected in the following way:

■ *1st gear*: Lift the top catch, pull the lever as far as possible towards the driver and push forwards.

■ *2nd, 3rd, 4th and 5th gears*: These can be selected from neutral without using either of the two catches.

■ *6th and 7th gears*: Lift both catches, pull the lever back as far as possible away from the driver, and push forward for the 7th gear.

■ *Reverse*: Lift both catches, pull the lever as far as possible towards the driver, and pull back.

Note: In order to select neutral from 6th, 7th or reverse gears, lift both catches. *Always* double de-clutch when changing up or down.

Steering

1) Forward left: Pull left-hand lever upwards until the spring-loaded plunger on the top of the lever locates in the notch on the curved guide. In this position, a radius or gradual turn to the left will be achieved. When the lever is pulled up further beyond the notch, a skid-turn to the left will be achieved. This is only effective when in low gear and at low speed.
2) Forward right: As for left steering but using the right-hand lever.
3) Reverse left (driving the rear of the tank to the left):
   a) Pull right-hand lever up to the radius position previously described, to obtain a gradual turn.
   b) Pull left-hand lever up to the skid position previously described, to obtain a skid-turn.
4) Reverse right (driving the rear of the tank to the right):
   a) Pull left-hand lever up to the radius position to obtain a gradual turn.
   b) Pull right-hand lever up to the skid position to obtain a skid-turn.
5) Neutral turn: When the tank is stationary with the engine running and the gear lever in neutral, a sharp pivot turn can be achieved by pulling either lever (according to which direction the turn is required) up to the radius position.

Braking

Although a footbrake is provided, a quicker stop can be achieved by pulling both steering levers up into the skid position, which gives the driver the benefit of the hydraulic pressure assistance.

Change down to a low gear when descending steep hills in order to conserve the life of the steering brake bands.

Driving controls

The driving controls for the driver were arranged as follows: the handbrake was the extreme left-hand lever with an exposed toothed track. There was a rod control to the steering brake bands. There were two steering levers, one on either side of the driver. These were pulled upwards towards the driver and operated hydraulic pressure to the steering brakes. This pressure was generated by two swash pumps, one for each steering brake, and were located under the turret basket on the left-hand side of the hull. The pumps were driven from the power take-off. The driver's gear lever was to be found on the left-hand side of the gearbox to the right of the driver. This lever was provided with two triggers – one at the top end and another at the lower end. First gear was selected by lifting the first trigger and thereafter from the second through to the seventh and reverse, it was necessary to lift both triggers together. The triggers control the amount of side movement of the gear lever when in neutral. At the bottom of the gear lever is a spring-loaded plunger which, when pulled towards the driver, allows the gear lever to crank to either a vertical or horizontal position. These were employed by the driver in the manner set out in the box, left.

BELOW The scene forward from mid-hull in a Panther. To the left is the driver's position. To the right that of the radio operator/gunner. The two large drumlike features cover the brakes for the drive sprocket.

ABOVE Not seen in the previous image is the frame that was mounted above the transmission that carried the Panther's radio(s). The fitment of both the standard FuG 5 and also a FuG 2 – the latter of which could only receive signals – indicates that this is the panzer of a company or platoon commander.

The radio fit

Apart from the more specialised radio fit to be found on the Panzerbefehlswagen Panther (Command Panther) and which is covered below, the standard radio fit for the Panther remained the same through all three production models.

Panthers serving with a platoon were each equipped with a single FuG 5 radio. This was a 10W dual transmitter with a very shortwave receiver with a range of between 4 and 6km dependent on prevailing weather conditions.

Platoon leader's panzers and those allocated to the company headquarters had a more complex radio fit given their command role. To the standard FuG 5 was added a FuG 2. The latter was a shortwave receiver which operated in the same frequency waveband as the FuG 5 of between 27.2 and 33.4MHz.

The FuG 5 radio was mounted on a frame that sat between the radio operator's position and the driver and on top of the transmission cover.

Vision devices

The specific vision devices for the driver and radio operator/machine gunner were determined by the mark of the Panther.

Initially, in the Ausf D, both the driver and radio operator each had a vision port controlled from the inside of the hull. Two fixed periscopes were also provided for the driver and were mounted above him in the hull roof plate, one giving vision straight ahead and the other to his half-left, which were used when the visor was closed down for combat. The radio operator also had two similar periscopes giving him vision straight ahead and half-right. This remained the same for the Ausf A as this later mark saw only changes to the turret.

With the introduction of the Ausf G in 1944, the driver's visor and that for the radio operator were deleted. The driver was now confined to a periscope mounted in the forward roof of the hull for external vision when closed down. This could pivot and was also traversable. It was covered and protected by an armoured cowl. This remained on all production Ausf Gs until the end of the conflict.

Escape hatches and fire extinguisher

Both positions are provided with escape hatches over their heads in the hull roof plate. Each can be unlocked from the inside by a small locking lever at the side, and can then be raised and swung round (this on the Ausfs D and A) on its spring-loaded column. The driver's hatch column is on the left and the radio operator's on the right. The hatches were balanced by the spring so that they were light and easy to operate. When fully opened the hatches engaged in locking catches mounted on the top of the hull roof plate on either side. These hatches could obviously be opened by either man in his position to provide extra ventilation.

A fire extinguisher for use within the hull was an automatically operated unit located in the centre of the engine bulkhead in the fighting compartment. This was automatically activated when the temperature rose above 120°F. A special quantity of extinguishing fluid lasting about 7 seconds was sprayed through jets on to the burning points. There was a red warning lamp on the instrument panel. This lit up when the extinguisher was in operation.

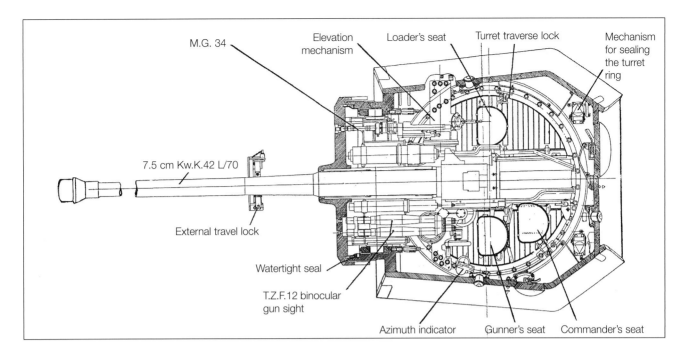

M.G. 34 — Elevation mechanism — Loader's seat — Turret traverse lock — Mechanism for sealing the turret ring

7.5 cm Kw.K.42 L/70

External travel lock

Watertight seal

T.Z.F.12 binocular gun sight

Azimuth indicator — Gunner's seat — Commander's seat

ABOVE Panther Ausf D turret before modification.

Part three: the turret and main armament

The turret and its armament were designed and produced by the company of Rheinmetall-Borsig AG, in Unterlüss, Niedersachsen, with the contract for the latter being issued by Wa Prüf 6 within weeks of the opening of the Russian Campaign. It proved to be the least problematic part of the Panther design, development and construction, and remained essentially the same in appearance until the end of the war. The Ausf F did feature a radical new turret but did not enter production before Germany surrendered, and therefore is not embraced by that observation.

Originally both the turret and the main gun were seen as an alternative to the Krupp-designed turret and weapon for the VK 45.01(P) and (H) designs – the tank that eventually became the Tiger I heavy tank.

In contradistinction to the Krupp turret, which was designed to house an 88mm L/56 gun, the specification issued to RM was to design a turret and its gun. This was required to penetrate 140mm of armour at 30 degrees at 100m range, but Wa Prüf 6 did not specify that the weapon be of 88mm calibre. Though the first gun built by RM and subsequently trialled was of an 75mm L/60 calibre, by the end of 1941 they had settled on a calibre of L/70. The

RM turret with the L/70 gun was initially the preferred type for the new heavy tank and as late as July 1942 the plan had been that only the first 100 Tiger Is would be equipped with the 88mm L/56 weapon and thereafter all new Tigers would be equipped with the RM turret and weapon. However, as the 88mm L/56 had recently shown its ability to penetrate 100mm of armour as per the original specification, this obviated the need to employ the RM turret and weapon for the heavy tank. Nevertheless, the demonstrated efficacy of the 75mm L/70 weapon had led to Wa Prüf 6 including it as the specified weapon for its VK 30.02. MAN adopted the RM turret and its gun as part of its submission for that programme from the outset. Thus, the production Panther employed a turret that was originally designed for the Tiger I.

The turret armour thickness and angles from the vertical as fitted to the Ausf D were as follows:

Turret roof	16mm	85–90 degrees
Turret front	100mm	10 degrees
Turret sides	45mm	25 degrees
Turret rear	45mm	25 degrees
Gun mantlet	100mm	Round

Note: Changes that occurred in production will be addressed in the section which looks at the individual models.

The gun mantlet straddled almost the full width of the turret front. It was a curved steel casting 100mm in thickness set at an angle of 12 degrees.

Combat experience indicated the vulnerability of the armour on the turret sides and of the 45mm superstructure sloping side armour. The following excerpt from a report detailing the Panther's combat debut at Kursk described a common experience for all Panthers until which time that the thickness of the superstructure sloping armour was raised by 10mm with the introduction of the

---

INSTRUCTIONS FOR TRAVERSING THE TURRET

Trainee Panther crew were inculcated with a number of procedures for operating the tank. The effectiveness of the Panther in combat was determined by adherence to these basic instructions.

1) During travelling and transport the main gun must be locked in the clamp. This would need to be released for operations.
2) Before operating the elevating and traversing gear, free the lock and turret seal.
3) Operate the hydraulic unit controls smoothly.
4) Handle the turret sighting mechanism with care.
5) When washing down, tighten the seals for the turret ring and the mantlet so that no water can get in (the need to provide effective waterproof seals for the mantlet was one of the reasons for the new turret on the Ausf A).
6) After washing down, take out the periscope prisms. Clean and dry.
7) Check the rubber seals every eight weeks (it was noted that the rubber could perish quite quickly, especially if the rubber employed was synthetic).
8) The following positions in the turret are provided with lubricating points and must be greased when necessary (to determine 'necessary' meant frequent checking):
   a) The turret traverse gearbox;
   b) traverse indicator; and
   c) turret lock.

Ausf G in 1944. Although it did not prevent an Ausf G being defeated by having its side armour penetrated, it did make it more problematic for the enemy to achieve this. Turret side armour, which was not increased on the Ausf G, remained as vulnerable. It began by noting:

Even direct hits from straight on fired from 76mm anti-tank and tank guns did not penetrate through the gun mantlet. However, the sides of the Panther were penetrated at ranges exceeding 1,000 metres. The 76mm anti-tank gun and tank rounds broke cleanly through the turret sides and both the sloped and vertical sides. In most cases, the Panther immediately caught fire. This was possibly due to the large amount of propellant in the ammunition that is carried.

Problems with the turret armour included those generated by the pistol port and the communications hatch. There had been occasions that, when hit, they recoiled inside the turret, injuring crew. Similar problems occurred with the turret hatch. It was unquestionably the case that the inclusion of both in the turret side armour led to the reduction in the armour's strength. The ports were deleted in December 1943, although the Ausf As built between September and December 1943 retained the pistol ports but not the communications hatch, which was discontinued from the outset.

It was noted, however, that there was a concern which was certainly translated into reality, becoming sufficiently so for it to lead to a change in the design of the mantlet on later Ausf Gs produced from September 1944 onward: '. . . Rounds hitting the lower half of the gun mantlet will be deflected downward and penetrate though the roof of the crew compartment.'

Indeed, in Normandy it became known to the British and Americans that aiming for the lower part of the mantlet was recommended to Allied tankers as a way of neutralising the Panther.

The turret had a carrier ring that rested on a turret race comprised of ball bearings which permitted a 360-degree traverse. The space between this ring and the external race on the hull could be sealed, if the Panther chose to wade a watercourse, by a steel band with rubber lining

LEFT In this view looking down through the space in the hull top that takes the turret, it is possible to see the double torsion bar system and the powertrain from the engine in the rear running through to the transmission. In the very centre is the turret-traversing motor.

which could be tightened by a lever. However, it was emphasised that this seal could only be tightened when the turret was locked.

Unlike the M4 or T-34, which employed electric motors to effect the traverse of the turret, that of the Panther employed a hydraulic 'turret drive'. This utilised a vertical shaft, hydraulic unit, a second shaft and a pair of bevel wheels to the clutch. In the event of the failure of this system there was a back-up in the form of an auxiliary turret traverse gear. This was situated on the right of the turret and was used by the loader for the assistance of the gunner when traversing the turret by hand.

The main gun

For German tankers in receipt of new Panthers, the most valued and reliable aspect of the design was the main armament, which proved itself very quickly to be far superior to the 75mm KwK L/48 mounted on the Panzer IV and StuG III. The main gun was undoubtedly the prime asset of the design and was to remain so to the end of the war. It was a semi-automatic weapon which was fired electrically with a high muzzle velocity and a flat trajectory. Indeed, so flat was

its trajectory that the gunner had no need to alter his elevation settings until he began to aim at targets in excess of 2,000m.

Even at the Battle of Kursk, where the performance of the new medium tank had been less than auspicious, there was unqualified praise for the accuracy and hitting power of the 75mm KwK42 L/70 high-velocity main gun. Indeed, in time it came to be known from prisoner interrogations that the Russians had acquired a great respect for the main armament of the Panther. A post-battle report sent to the OKH was most succinct: 'No real complaints. Frequently achieved hits on T-34 tanks at over 3,000-metres range.'

Despite the rather lacklustre perceived performance of the Panther during the Kursk offensive, it still managed to claim 263 Russian tanks destroyed by 19 July.

The main gun was officially designated as the 75mm KwK42 L/70. The barrel of the weapon was machined in one piece with a removable breech plate. This was mounted on, and adjusted by, the cradle within the turret. At the muzzle end of the barrel of 70 calibres' length was a baffle which functioned as a muzzle

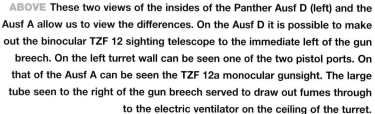

ABOVE These two views of the insides of the Panther Ausf D (left) and the Ausf A allow us to view the differences. On the Ausf D it is possible to make out the binocular TZF 12 sighting telescope to the immediate left of the gun breech. On the left turret wall can be seen one of the two pistol ports. On that of the Ausf A can be seen the TZF 12a monocular gunsight. The large tube seen to the right of the gun breech served to draw out fumes through to the electric ventilator on the ceiling of the turret.

brake to help neutralise the recoil when fired. Indeed, up to 70% of the recoil was soaked up when the explosive gases omitted by the shell struck the baffle's break plates inside the muzzle brake and then vented out of the sides. This prevented the recoil within the turret from being excessive. It was for this reason that the gun could not be fired without the muzzle brake attached to the barrel.

In a conference held at Kummersdorf on 25 October 1944, it was critically noted that the Panther had a rate of fire *significantly* lower than that of the US M4 tank. This same matter was picked up once again after the war by the French Army, who employed the Panther and Jagdpanther in limited numbers and produced *Le Panther 1947*, a remarkably objective document, in which they made the following observation: 'Once the commander has located a target, it takes between 20 and 30 seconds until the gunner can open fire.' Attributing this delay to 'the absence of a periscope for the gunner'.

Although the gunner had his own periscope gunsight – which was deemed to be excellent – the reference is to the fact that he had no other type of observation device. In consequence, the gunner was, to all intents and purposes, practically blind. This was assessed by the French evaluation team that compiled *Le Panther 1947* to be one of its greatest shortcomings. Even then, it was also noted that: 'During a rapid rate of fire – 20 rounds per minute was only permissible in exceptional cases when circumstances so dictate – it is not uncommon to be forced to break off firing when the recoil of the gun has reached its permissible limit (cease fire).'

The French were sufficiently impressed by the Panther's 75mm L/70 main gun to adopt it, albeit in a modified form, to equip their own domestically produced AMX 13 light tank developed from the late 1940s. This same weapon then found its way on to a modified version of the M4 employed by the Israeli Army in the 1950s and '60s.

When the Panther was not in combat and the main gun was in the travelling position – no depression or elevation – it was locked in place by being secured to a clamp, which was hinged to the front superstructure roof.

Vision devices for the main gun

The optics fitted to German tanks were always of the highest quality and those of the Panther were no different. Soviet tankers readily acknowledged the optics' superior class and in addition there is a classic example of a British tank crew who employed a captured Panther against its former owners late in 1944, and who praised their quality, being superior to that fitted to their own machines.

During the course of its production life the Panther was equipped with two types of gunsight. From the start of production through to late November/early December 1943 all Ausf Ds and the first tranche of Ausf As were equipped with a binocular TZF 12 sight. Thereafter, all Panthers were equipped with a monocular TZF 12a sight. Both of these sights were mounted such that they were parallel with the main gun. In the case of the former:

Each of the two sight tubes had a different sight reticule. The pattern on the left reticule consisted of 7 triangles, separated by 4 mils. Placing the target on the point of a triangle allowed the gunner to aim without obstructing the view of the target. The distances between triangles were used to lead moving targets. The triangle height and separation distances in mils were also used as an aid in estimating the range to a target. The pattern in the right reticule also contained the 7 triangles plus adjustable range scales that allowed the gunner to register the exact range to the target. The range scale was graduated at 100-metre intervals out to a range of 2,000 metres for the Pzgr.40/42, 3,000 metres for the Pzgr. 39/42 and 4,000 metres for the Sprgr.42.

The introduction of the monocular TZF 12a sight on to the Ausf A in November/December 1943 was a simpler sight introduced as much to preserve resources as it was to enable it to be easy to operate for the gunner. Combat experience had shown the need for the gunner's sight to have a wider view to locate targets. This was aided by the provision of a scale magnification of ×2.5. For longer-range targets the gunner could switch to a ×5 magnification. In either case, it was possible for the gunner to register the exact range to the target. The range scale was adjusted in the same fashion as the TZF 12 for the ammunition types.

Ammunition types

The authorised maximum load for ammunition was 79 rounds, but this did not prevent tank crews from loading more when going into combat. Three types of ammunition were carried.

1) Panzergranate (Pzgr) 39/42
14.3kg shell with a length of 893mm.
This was the standard anti-tank ammunition carried by the Panther. It had a compressed charge which imparted a high muzzle velocity of 925m/sec. Commander and gun aimer could gauge the direction of travel by the fact that once fired it emitted a 2-second burn of tracer, permitting them to make corrections if they were needed for the next shot.

As the purpose of this particular ammunition was to effect the destruction of the enemy tank by generating severe damage within its interior, the size of the HE part of the shell was not large, as its modus operandi was to penetrate the armour of the enemy machine without causing a premature detonation in the process. Hence the position of the detonating fuse at the base of the shell. Normally some 40 rounds of the two types of armour-piercing rounds (Pzgr 39/42 and a smaller number of Pzgr 40/42) were carried in a normal load.

2) Pzgr 40/42
11.2kg shell with a length of 929mm.
The carriage of a small number of high-performance, very high-velocity armour-piercing rounds was a feature of certain tanks in the conflict. The T-34 was equipped with a special 76.2cm shell with a tungsten core as was the high-velocity armour-piercing (HVAP) 76mm-armed US M4. Such a round in the British Army received the designation APCR (standing for armour-piercing composite rigid). That of the Panther was designated as the Pzgr 40/42. It had an exceedingly high muzzle velocity of 1,120m/sec and its design was characterised by a lightweight metal outer body encasing a

RIGHT An example of the main armour-piercing shell (Pzgr 39/42) carried by the Panther. This shell had a velocity of 3,068ft per second, which enabled it to penetrate the frontal armour on almost all enemy tanks at battle ranges.

sub-calibre tungsten core. The two elements, once fired from the Panther's gun, flew to the target, whereupon the outer body shell peeled away and allowed the dense sub-calibre core to penetrate the armour of the enemy tank. However, it was noted that the aerodynamic properties of this shell caused the range to fall off over distance, lowering its muzzle velocity. This resulted in a drop in the kinetic energy potential of the tungsten core and thus of its penetrative capabilities. It was primarily employed against the more heavily armoured Soviet heavy tanks and assault gun derivatives.

3) Sprenggrenate 42

11kg shell with a length of 876mm.
This was a high-explosive fragmentation round with a lower muzzle velocity – 701m/sec – than the two armour-piercing rounds. It would be employed against 'softer' targets and proved the round of choice to be used against sited anti-tank guns and transport vehicles. Approximately 32 rounds of the type of ammunition was carried in a normal Panther load.

Ammunition stowage

According to Dr Wiebecke, the Chief Engineer of the Panther at MAN, it was the OKH itself that had responsibility for the design of 'the stowage arrangements [of the Panther] and had furnished this information to MAN for incorporation in the production drawings'. It would seem this extended to the stowage of ammunition within the Panther.

There was little significant change to the manner in which ammunition was stowed across all three of the Panther variants. On the Ausf G – which is the subject of the walk-around in Chapter 4 – there was provision for a total of 82 rounds. However, unlike in the later M4, this ammunition was not stored in armoured or protected bins. They were thus vulnerable – especially the 24 rounds stored on the right side of the hull and the 28 on the left. There were also a further 4 rounds located next to the driver's position. It is worth noting at this point that although the M4 had a reputation of 'brewing up', acquiring the derogatory monikers of 'Tommy Cooker' and 'Ronson Lighter', the Panther was not immune to such a fiery fate. In Chapter 5, there is a short account by a young SS Panther commander serving in Normandy, whose tank was disabled by a mine and enemy anti-tank fire. Having just bailed out of his charge, he reports: 'I saw flames coming out of my hatch as if from a blowtorch.' Guderian also made reference in a report from Normandy on the tendency of the Panther 'to catch fire'.

The British Army conducted a whole raft of tests and evaluations of the Panther after the war and in one, entitled *Military Operational Research Report No. 61 Study No. 11 Motion Studies of German Tanks*, held in the Tank Museum, the author, one Captain G. Tunnicliffe, writing in 1947, described the four ammunition racks (in British parlance – panniers) accessible by the loader in a Panther Ausf G. This last variant carried three more rounds of main ammunition when compared to the 79 on the Ausfs D and A.

Racks A, B, C and D are the four pannier racks, which are accessible from the turret. Each rack holds twelve rounds, stowed horizontally. The four rounds in the bottom layer are stowed bases rear, the three rounds in the next layer base forward and the top layer of two rounds is stowed base forward. . . . Each layer is supported by two steel arms, each of which is hinged and

RIGHT **This image illustrates the size of the Pzgr 39/42. Its weight of 14kg or 31lb was quite heavy, so the process of rearming a Panther – and this might occur a number of times in an ongoing battle – could of itself be very tiring for the crew.**

RIGHT A view from within the turret basket taking in the loader's and commander's positions. Under the commander's seat can be seen a vertical bin with more main gun ammunition located on clips attached to the sponson walls.

springs upwards when the layer of rounds is removed from it. This facilitates access to the layer below.

Later, in this same report, Tunnicliffe drew attention to an aspect of the ammunition storage that to British eyes was poorly designed and potentially problematic in a combat situation:

There are four vertical storage racks accessible to the loader: they are rack E, F, G, and H and contain a total of 19 stowed rounds, all stowed base down. The racks are similar in design, and are built of sheet metal. The rounds are held by base cups and double top flaps which hinge inwards and which, when closed, hold rounds rigid.

. . . a further bad feature was that when the flaps were opened and the first round removed, there was no support for the remaining rounds and they were liable to fall over. When this happened, they were however not only difficult to find and reach but would have also jammed the turret had it been suddenly traversed.

It must be assumed that this did happen on occasions and this was a contingency that experienced crews knew how to deal with. It was also the case that crews might choose to load more than the standard load if heavy combat was in the offing. Like refuelling, reloading ammunition in the midst of battle was always a risky operation.

RIGHT Seen in this image are two bins for vertically stored 75mm ammunition. Also seen is the manner in which boxes for the two MG 34s were carried between the front of the turret basket on the left and the driver's and radio operator's positions. These contained the 4,800 rounds of MG ammunition carried by a Panther.

ABOVE Ammunition stowage seen from the commander's seat. It is worth noting that by this stage of the war the need to preserve copper and zinc saw the replacement of brass for most shell casings by steel that had been lacquered (as can be clearly seen on these 75mm shells). Some 82 main rounds were carried by the Ausf G.

Chapter Four

Panther walk-around

The Panther Ausf G that is the subject of this 'walk-around' is to be found in the Tank Museum at Bovington, Dorset, in the UK. It is not a runner, unlike some held by other museums and in private collections.

OPPOSITE The Tank Museum's Panther Ausf G. *(Shutterstock)*

All photographs in this chapter were taken by the Tank Museum's official photographer, except for those supplied by Thomas Anderson, whose images are credited 'TA'.

1 This particular example of the Panther Ausf G was never employed in combat. It was one of nine found partially completed on the production line at MNH at the end of the war and was finished, along with a number of others, with the assistance of German workers by the 823 Armoured Troop of the Royal Electrical Mechanical Engineers (REME) No 8, British Army of the Rhine (BAOR), in 1945. It had been allotted the Fahrgestellnummer 129113. It was thus not only one of the last produced before the end of the war, but it would also have been one of the very last Panthers to have been manufactured before production of the type was to have been closed down by the Germans themselves under the Emergency Panzer Programme promulgated in January 1945. We have taken advantage of

the provision of colour pictures supplied by Mr Thomas Anderson of the Panther Ausf G held at the Bundeswehr Tank Museum at Münster, and also the Panther Ausf A held at Koblenz, to help offer contrast with aspects of the Bovington Panther. It is painted to represent the camouflage scheme worn by Panthers towards the very end of the war.

We begin with the turret and move down to the hull and then to the chassis.

2 Moving from left to right across the image can be seen the thin metal debris guard covering the gap between the turret and mantlet. Clearly seen are the three welded threaded sockets fitted from June 1944, that enabled troops to erect a *Behelfskran*, a 2-ton crane to help effect repairs to the tank, such as

removal of the transmission. Fitted on all marks of the Panther was an exhaust fan protected by an armoured guard. This armoured guard was originally of a welded design but in July 1944 it was replaced by a cast cover which was retained until the end of the war. However, some Panthers were still fitted with the earlier design until supplies had run out.

To the right of the cupola can be seen the external cover for the *Nahverteidigungswaffe* – the close defence weapon – that was loaded from within the turret. There are also the three lifting eyes on the turret. The only change between the turret fitted to the Ausf A and the Ausf G was the small triangular brace welded to the rearmost lifting eye to give it greater strength.

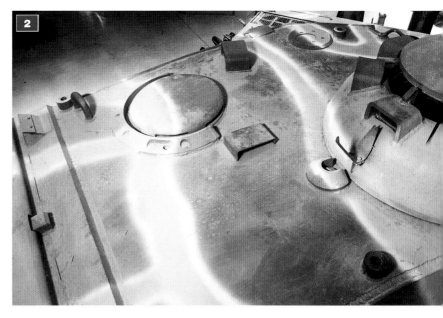

3 The cast cupola of 100mm thickness was first introduced on the Panther with the Ausf A in September 1943. It was equipped to receive seven glass periscopes with a number of replacements available to hand for the tank commander in the event of one or more of them being damaged by enemy fire (although these are absent from this example). The cast cupola with its periscopes gave the tank commander a superior view of the battlefield environment when compared to the drum-type cupola of the Ausf A. Note also the sighting

vane which is fitted to a mounting bracket on the new cupola. This feature was first seen on the Ausf A and was retained on all Panthers through to the end of the war. There is also a new periscope for the gun loader; before this was fitted, he was blind to events beyond the turret. He was therefore now in a position to assist the tank commander in the acquisition of targets and be aware of the immediate tactical situation. In January 1945, the addition of the ring to permit the carriage of an anti-aircraft gun from the cupola was deleted.

4 & 5 Drawing on the colour images of the Koblenz Ausf G, it is possible to get a better perspective on the mounting of the FG1250 infra-red searchlight and scope that started to be fitted to Panthers in small numbers beginning in September 1944. Had the war continued and production of this equipment been maintained, it was the intention to fit as many Panthers as possible with these devices to enable more fighting to be done at night and away from overwhelming Allied daytime air power. *(Thomas Anderson – TA)*

6 Seen mounted on the cupola ring of the Münster Ausf A is the *Fliegerbeschussgerät* (anti-aircraft mount) for an MG 34. When not in use, the gun was carried internally and the mount, which when in use was able to slide around the ring, was locked in place to avoid movement. *(TA)*

7 Seen face-on, albeit looking only at the right-hand side of the gun mantlet, the monocular TZF 12a gunsight can clearly be seen, as can the driver's vision block mounted on the roof of the hull. The monocular gunsight was first introduced on the Ausf A in November/December 1943. The nature of the Zimmerit pattern identifies this as a MAN-produced Panther. *(TA)*

8 & 9 These images are of the left- and right-hand sides of the mantlet of Münster's Ausf A. The shape of the new mantlet casting distinguished it from that of the earlier Ausf D. Most prominent are the square-cut, interlocked turret side plates which are in contrast to the earlier dovetailed cut of the Ausf D. This new form of mantlet and turret was retained through to the end of Panther production, albeit with minor changes. *(TA)*

9a

9a The rear of the turret of the Ausf G was carried over from the Ausf A, except that in June 1944 a handle was welded on the outside of the circular access/escape hatch in response to user complaints that it could not be opened from the outside and also quite often, did not fully engage with the turret when closed.

10 The single Bosch headlight on the Ausf D, which was emplaced on the right of the glacis, was carried over to the Ausf A, as seen here on the Münster Panther. What can also be seen is the driver's visor built into the hull glacis, a feature deleted on the Ausf G. *(TA)*

11 On the Ausf G this was changed with the headlight being moved and fixed directly on to the mudguard over the front of the track.

10

11

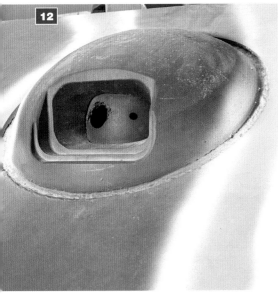

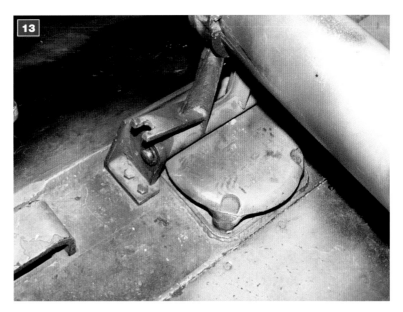

12 A major change introduced in late November/December 1943 – dependent on manufacturer – was the deletion of the 'letterbox' flap for the hull machine gun and its replacement with a far better-protected and more sophisticated ball-mount for the onboard hull MG 34.

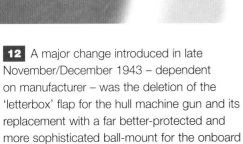

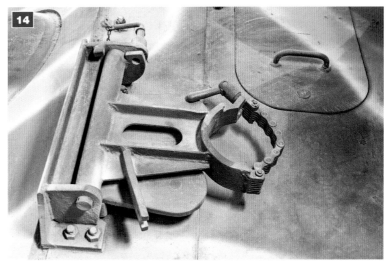

13 & 14 Common to all variants of the Panther was the travel lock for the main gun under which was located a ventilator cover, seen here on the Ausf A. When not in use the travel lock lay flat on the hull roof, as is seen on the Ausf G.

14a Seen from the turret is the driver's station in the roof of the hull of the Koblenz Ausf G. This clearly shows the major change in the hatches from the Ausf A. The 'lift-up and swivel hatches' were replaced by those that were hinged to open up at 90 degrees. To close, the driver (and radio operator, for his was of the same type) reached over and grabbed the rod that can be seen on the inside of the hatch and pulled it closed. This could place a physical strain on either crewman as they would need to make much more effort to do so than with the earlier type hatch. Also clearly seen is the driver's rotatable periscope that replaced the visor in the glacis on the Ausf A, as well as his leather padded seat within the hull. *(TA)*

15 A characteristic feature of all three models of the Panther were the stowage racks fixed on the hull sides on which various tools and other items were carried. A number of different types of these brackets were fitted and they differed between manufacturers. The projecting lugs were designed to house the towing shackles.

16 & 17 Carried on all Panther models was the gun-cleaning tube, wherein were housed the elements that formed the main gun-cleaning device. The manner in which the tube was itself divided into two sections can be seen in the second image. A number of tank crews chose to relocate the gun cleaning tube and fitted it so that it was mounted across the rear of the hull deck.

18 A more detailed view of the equipment fitted on the stowage rack of the Panther underneath the radio operator's hatch. It can clearly be seen how the S-shaped towing shackles were retained on the forward part of the bracket, while to the rear is a Tetra fire extinguisher and below it an axe. The stowage racks fitted to the Ausf G were as those on the Bergepanther. *(TA)*

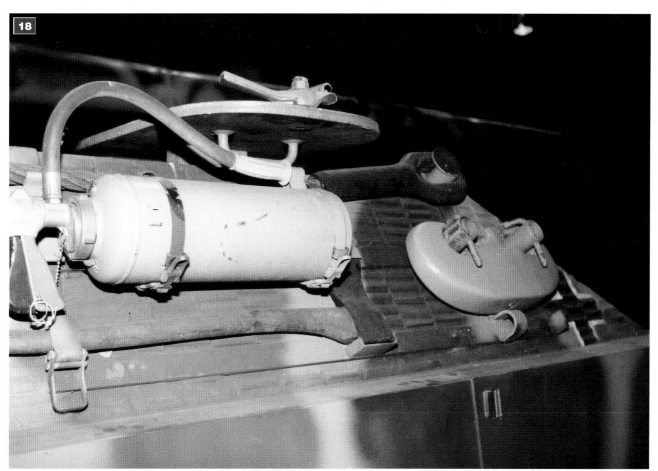

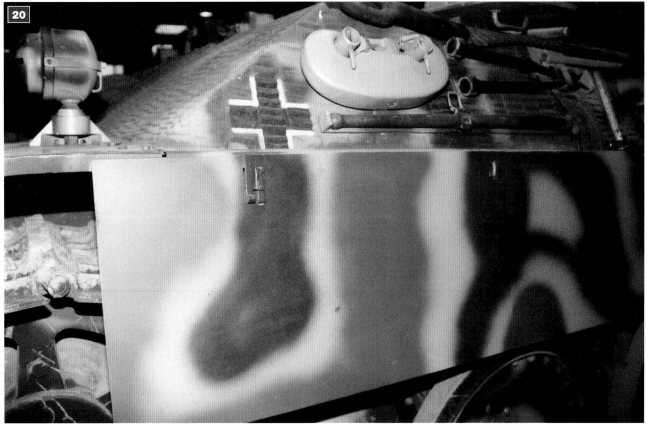

19 Back to the other side of the hull of the Koblenz Ausf G. This has been included because it has a more complete fit of equipment. To the fore is another towing shackle and behind it a heavy-duty wire-cutter. There is also a spade. At the top of the hull is the towing cable, which on this example is to be seen on both sides of the hull running for its full length. Underneath the brackets can be seen the Zimmerit finish. *(TA)*

20 The *Schürzen* – skirts – were made of soft steel and were introduced on the Panther early on in the production run of the Ausf D. It was counter-intuitive that such thin plates could protect the inner hull from hits from 75mm fire but they did so, as they did against the fire of massed Soviet anti-tank rifles. It was the success of this particular solution to the armour problem of the Panther that led to the demise of the Panther II. One of their failings was that the mountings were too flimsy and were easily lost on Ausf Ds and As in close country. *(TA)*

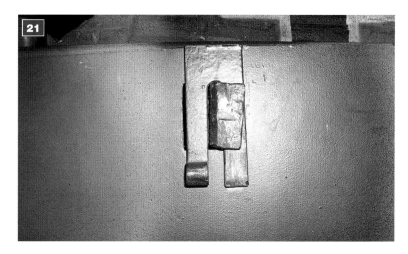

21 This shows how the *Schürzen* were hung from the brackets attached to the undersides of the hull sponsons on the first two marks of the Panther. *(TA)*

22 On the Ausf G, the *Schürzen* were mounted on hangers that were now welded to a rigid horizontal strip running nearly the full length of the new hull side armour. This permitted them to withstand greater stress, but it did not mean that they never came away in combat.

23 Viewed from the top of the turret is the rear hull of the Tank Museum Panther. Moving forward from the rear it can be seen that a number of the armoured covers are missing, in particular the armoured cowl over the air intake. This, however, can be seen in the next image.

24 The rear of the Koblenz Ausf G clearly shows those elements missing from that of the Bovington Panther. Also much in evidence are the *Flammvernichter* – exhaust mufflers – that were designed to disguise the intense glow from the exhaust pipes of the Panther at night. *(TA)*

25 Beginning in October 1944, all new-build Panthers were equipped with a *Warmluftbeheizung* – a warm air heater. The warm air was diverted into the crew

25

compartment by a fan. This was enclosed in the low tower that stood proud of the rear hull deck of the tank. The hole is where the radio antenna would normally have been fitted.

26 This image gives a complete sweep across the rear of the engine deck of the Koblenz Ausf G. All of the grilles are screened and the radio aerial in its antenna foot is clearly to be seen. On either side of the upper hull are two towing cables which lie above the spare tracks. This Panther was built after October 1944 as it does not wear Zimmerit. In December 1944, metal covers using the material employed for *Schürzen* were placed above the intake and exhaust grilles on the rear deck of Panthers to protect them from shrapnel and shell splinters. *(TA)*

26

27 A more complete view of the rear of the hull. Between the two exhaust mufflers is to be seen the vehicle jack stowed in the vertical position. This had been changed, as on the Ausf D the jack was located beneath the exhausts and stored horizontally. This Ausf G differs to the example at Bovington in that it still retains the cast bases to the exhaust pipes. *(TA)*

28 A close-up of the top of the exhaust muffler of the Bovington Ausf G. Its purpose was to substantially reduce the red-hot glow that emanated from the top of the exhaust pipes of the Panther at night. This was deemed to be a sufficiently negative aspect of the Panther's operation that it was mentioned as such in a US Army report on the tank.

29 On the rear hull plate of the Koblenz Ausf G can be seen the covers over the track tensioners, the two S-type towing shackles and the larger towing shackle fitted to the circular engine access hatch. *(TA)*

30 Introduced towards the end of August/beginning of September 1944, was a new rear stowage box design peculiar to MNH and seen

here on the Bovington Panther built by that company. It employed a stamped face with five vertical ribs in contradistinction to those fitted by the other companies building both the Panther and Jagdpanther, which used stowage boxes with a stamped, ribbed 'X' design. Whereas the Koblenz Ausf G is fitted with cast armour guards at the base of the exhaust pipes, the Bovington Ausf G has had those replaced by welded armour guards.

31 Unlike the rear idler which was changed on the Ausf G, the front drive sprocket retained the same design throughout the production life of the Panther.

32 For the greater period of its production life the Panther was equipped with two small rubber-tyred rollers that were located behind the drive sprockets – one on either side. They were there to prevent the track doubling up on itself when the tank was reversing. *(TA)*

33 It was only very late in the production life of the Ausf G that the rubber-tyred wheel was replaced by a solid metal *Gleitschuh* – skid shoe. This was a contingency generated by the declining supplies of rubber in the closing months of the war.

34 The rubber-tyred road wheels of the Panther were problematic throughout its career. Initially it was to do with the number of rim bolts employed to secure the solid rubber tyres. Originally there were just 16, but by August 1943 this had been increased to 24. *(TA)*

35 The greatest benefit of the interleaved road wheel suspension was the stability of the drive it conveyed for the crew when moving across country. Its downside was the need to have to remove outer road wheels to gain access to the inner run if one or more failed.

36 When the Ausf G went into production in April 1944 at MAN, and thereafter with the other producers, all except DB employed a new cast idler. Of 650mm diameter it had been designed to be self-cleaning, thereby preventing the build-up of mud and snow that otherwise had to be cleared by hand. DB, however, retained the earlier idler design on the Ausf Gs they produced.

37 The tracks on the Panther each comprised 87 links secured by dry single link pins. These made them fairly easy to replace. From September 1943 tracks were cast with six *stollen* – chevrons – on to the face of the track to facilitate better grip in Russian mud and snow. The length of the track when on the ground was 12ft 9½in. Spare tracks were carried along the rear part of the sloping hull as well as on the turret sides. This was more a choice of the tank crew as, when placed there, they were effectively doubling up as extra armour.

Chapter Five

Panther at war

─(●)──────────

The Panther first saw service in Russia at the Battle of Kursk in July 1943, although its combat debut was less than auspicious. Later, it also saw service in Italy and Western Europe after D-Day. Panthers generated a reputation on all battlefronts as formidable and dangerous opponents, but their performance was hamstrung by technical problems that were not cured before the end of the conflict.

OPPOSITE March 1944 saw the first commitment of the Panther beyond the Russian theatre when the newly formed 1/Pz.Rgt 4 was sent from France to Italy. A Panther of this formation passes the Colosseum in Rome.

The purpose of this chapter is to offer an insight into the Panther at war. Given that it served on all the major fronts that the German Army was fighting on from the summer of 1943 to the end of the conflict in Europe, it will not be possible to provide a detailed coverage of *all* the operations in which it participated in the short space that is available in this book. I have thus sought to give insight into the manner in which the German armed forces employed it by focusing on a number of these – both East and West – to act as exemplars. We begin, however, with that which witnessed its combat debut in the summer of 1943 in Russia.

'Our problem child'

Unternehmen *Zitadelle* (Operation Citadel) – the codename for the planned German offensive against the Kursk salient in eastern Ukraine – had optimistically been scheduled to begin 'as soon as the ground was dry' in May 1943. And while Hitler had ordered in June of the previous year that 250 of the new Panthers had to be available to participate in the operation, even as the first delayed examples came off the production lines in Germany, it became very apparent that this new panzer was in no state to enter combat that quickly as it was displaying a plethora of teething troubles. That it took until July before *Zitadelle* was launched was primarily due to the offensive being repeatedly postponed in order to solve the ongoing problems with the new machine.

As we have seen, the hope that MAN and DB would have produced the first production examples of the Panther before the end of 1942 had been thwarted due to problems with setting up the production lines, assuring supplies of materials and other equipment and the general rapidity with which this whole complex programme was being pushed. The imperative to get this new medium panzer into production as soon as possible necessarily brought such problems in its train. In January 1943, just four examples of the Ausf D had been completed by MAN, followed by a further 18 by MAN, DB and MNH in February. Only in March did the numbers start to rise to a level commensurate with expectations. MAN produced 25 (but none in April), DB 14, MNH 26 and Henschel came

on line with its first 26. By May, the total number of Panthers that had been manufactured by the four companies had reached 324. However, so extensive were the problems evidenced by the new tank and so great the priority of the Panther programme that the *Waffenamt* took the radical decision that, from April, all new-build Panthers leaving their respective production lines would automatically be despatched via the Reichsbahn to the Demag works at Falkensee in Berlin for rebuilding at an overhaul facility set up for the task. The consequent slippage of the programme to account for this resulted in the first of a series of delays to the timetable for the launch of *Zitadelle*, which Hitler was not prepared to launch without the Panther being present.

In anticipation of receipt of the new tank, the Army had raised its first Panther battalion on 9 January 1943 at Erlangen. A second followed on 6 February. These received the designations *Panzer Abteilungen* 51 and 52, with each due to receive 96 of the new panzer with initial deliveries planned to begin to the former at the end of January. It would be these two formations that would take the Panther into action at Kursk. These two units had been allocated the first 20 Panthers, produced with the original 60mm armoured glacis and the HL 210 engine. Following the Führer conference on 5 May, in which Hitler had once more asserted that participation of the Panther was essential to ensure the success of *Zitadelle*, he ordered that the two battalions be returned from France to train at the Army Training Ground at Grafenwöhr, some 88km north-east of Nuremberg. Six days later, Guderian was in Berlin to discuss the continuing development issues of what he had come to call 'our problem child'. It was apparent that the 250 machines Hitler had stipulated be ready for May could not be achieved, as only about 100 were available. Nonetheless, with pressure building to have these first two battalions ready for *Zitadelle*, they now received absolute priority in the allocation of all rebuilds, with the first 192 from this programme being despatched to Grafenwöhr by the end of that month. Those formerly employed by the battalions for training were to be handed back and sent for rebuilding in their turn.

As the personnel of *Abteilungen* 51 and 52 worked up on their revamped charges, they had been visited by Guderian on 1 June where it became apparent to him that despite the rebuilds there were still ongoing problems with the panzers. It is the measure of just how extensive and persistent these were that it was now realised that if these two formations were to be available for the offensive at all, it would only be by recourse to yet another emergency rebuild, and on site at Grafenwöhr. So pressing was the need to get them ready, that even Panther crews were drafted in to work alongside those from the manufacturing companies to deal with problems continuing to plague mainly the Panther's engine, the transmission, fuel pumps and road wheels. But perhaps the greatest problem to flow from the use of the tank crews themselves in this work was the inability to find the time to undergo their indoctrination and training sessions on their new charges. This is perhaps best described in the words of a tanker from 4/Pz.Abt 51:

Training on the Panther was more than inadequate. Non-available training material and unschooled teachers resulted in only 60% training on the Panther and the rest on the Panzer IV. After receiving the Panther we had a short driver training period. Then started the big modifications programme on the Panthers at Grafenwöhr in which we all participated. All the modifications were to be made under time pressure. The crew had no Panzers nor did they get live fire training. Unit training was not performed either.

Whereas this may have been alleviated had the crews been wholly drawn from experienced combat veterans, this was not the case due to Hitler's insistence that new equipment was allocated to new and 'green' formations. Although

ABOVE The ongoing problems with the first tranche of Panther Ausf Ds destined for service in the *Zitadelle* offensive saw a second 'emergency' rebuild at the Army Training Ground at Grafenwöhr in the early spring of 1943. This was carried out, in the main in the open, in very unfavourable weather conditions. Eleven Panthers can be seen here. *(Author)*

ABOVE Movement orders for the Panthers of *Abteilungen* 51 and 52 came towards the end of June 1943.

PANZER DIVISION 43 AND THE PANTHER

In keeping with the appointment of General Heinz Guderian as Inspector General of Panzer Troops, armed with the brief from Hitler to revamp the armoured force into 'a war-winning weapon', it was formally renamed and from thence forward became the *Panzerwaffe*. This was a far-ranging change because above all it saw the creation of a new panzer division structure. Under the heading of Panzer Division 43 it was an attempt to streamline the divisional structure with the new Panther medium tank at the heart of this change.

Each panzer division would now have one panzer regiment made up of two battalions, with each battalion in its turn consisting of four companies. Each company was to have an establishment of 22 tanks. The theory was that these would be composed only of the Panther, but this took no account of the reality of production, which in the case of the new medium tank was much slower than anticipated. The only recourse was to have one battalion equipped with the Panther and the other the Panzer Mark IV. By this date the G and later H models of this venerable, but still effective design were armed with a 75mm KwK40 L/48 main gun (early Gs were armed with the 75mm L/43, while production shifted to the longer weapon in March 1943).

This was viewed as an expedient. However, the war situation never reached a point where there were sufficient Panthers produced to do anything other than convert the first battalion of each panzer division with Panthers or supply new-builds as replacements for those lost in combat. Even then, the provision of 22 Panthers per battalion could not be realised because of the aforementioned problems and the number was perforce reduced to 17 Panthers per company by hiving off one platoon (*zug*). These were then available to be allocated to other units.

There would be other changes to the organisation of the *Panzerwaffe* before the end of the war to accommodate the realities of massive losses and declining manpower.

Abteilungen 51 and 52 had been formed around a small cadre of veteran officers and NCOs from the aforementioned panzer divisions, the bulk of the manpower were 'green troops' with negligible combat experience. Nonetheless, with the start date for *Zitadelle* having been finally set by him for 5 July, the Panther battalions received their movement orders.

Beginning on 24 June, the Panthers of *Abteilung* 51 were loaded aboard trains, with *Abteilung* 52 following a few days later. This process involved a total of 200 machines comprising 196 battle tanks and 4 recovery Bergepanthers. A measure of the technical problems still attending a large number of these new panzers was that mechanics and crew members were changing final drives on some of the Panthers even as they were en route to Eastern Ukraine on the rail flatbeds of the Reichsbahn.

Into combat – the Panther at Kursk

The German offensive began on 5 July and ended on the 17th when Hitler ordered it closed down. It was a decisive defeat for the Germans which led to the strategic initiative on the Eastern Front passing to the Red Army. Although the Germans had amassed a huge concentration of armour for the operation, which included the new Panther and a large number of Tigers and Ferdinand tank destroyers, they were unable to break the Soviet defences. What is presented below is not a detailed treatment of the battle, but rather a short analysis of the performance of the Panther in it.

The arrival of Panzer Regiment (Pz.Rgt) 39, comprising Battalions 51 and 52, in Russia was hardly auspicious as two of the new tanks burnt out on the drive to their assembly areas. For the purposes of the offensive, Pz.Rgt 39

was subordinated to the *Grossdeutschland* (GD) Panzer Grenadier Division, where combined with its own Pz.Rgt which was fielding 184 panzers and assault guns being redesignated Panzer Brigade 10 early on the morning of the offensive. On paper, Pz.Brig 10 was a formidable assemblage of armour and much was expected of it. Together with two other panzer divisions, they collectively formed 48th Panzer Corps, this constituting the single most powerful formation the Germans committed in the offensive. It was for that reason it had been set the objective of seeking a rapid breakthrough of the Soviet defences and the seizure of the bridge over the river Psel, roughly halfway to Kursk, in two days – a trifling distance when compared to earlier summer offensives. It was also tasked with protecting the extending flank of II SS Panzer Corps on its right wing as it drove towards the river Psel and then swung to the north-east towards Prokhorovka.

BELOW Each of the two *Abteilungen* were allocated two turretless Panthers each to function as Bergepanthers for the offensive.

ABOVE Very likely taken by a Leica camera belonging to a crewman of one of the three Panthers in the image, here we see preparations for battle in the remaining hours before the beginning of the offensive.

LEFT Panthers driving to a Russian village to their assembly point. For the purposes of the offensive the two Panther *Abteilungen* had been subordinated to the *Grossdeutschland* Panzer Grenadier Division, which was itself part of the 48th Panzer Corps.

ABOVE Panthers alongside armour of Panzer Grenadier Division *Grossdeutschland*. GD was unique among Army divisions committed to *Zitadelle* in having its own organic Tiger I company. Also to be seen with other Panthers in the background are Panzer IIIs – in actuality the most numerous German tank in the operation.

But the Kursk battlefield was unlike any the *Panzerwaffe* had ever faced before and even the sheer weight of German armour, including the much hoped-for Panther, could not neutralise the Red Army fighting a battle on its strongest terms – that of conducting a huge strategic defence. By the time the offensive was closed down 13 days later, 48th Panzer Corps was still many miles from achieving this its initial objective. Massive and numerous Soviet minefields, large

LEFT A Panther in its element! This is what the new medium tank was designed for – long-range fire across the steppe. It was under such conditions that a Panther destroyed a T-34 at some 3,000m range.

RIGHT Here we see a small collection of Red Army troopers resting in the lee of a Panther. Note the smoke candles – already deleted on Panthers being produced back in Germany.

BELOW A Panther bypassing a Henschel Type 33 Army truck on the main street of one of the many Russian villages that pock-marked the battlefield.

RIGHT A Panther bypasses a Panzer III with *Schürzen* around the turret belonging to the 11th Pz.Div.

BELOW The seemingly open countryside in front of these German panzers is deceptive. The Russians had laid huge minefields and stationed very large numbers of 76.2mm anti-tank guns in extremely well-camouflaged positions.

lines of hidden anti-tank guns and ferocious artillery barrages all sought to delay the German advance. This was then assailed by almost continual large-scale tank attacks on its extending left flank, which repeatedly diverted armour away from the main *schwerpunkt* (main target) to deal with them. Being unable to resolve this problem saw the bulk of the German mobile forces from 48th Panzer Corps tied down to the end of the offensive, contending with and unable to decisively defeat them. For a much more detailed coverage of the battle, see my book, *Zitadelle* (2008).

That the Panther did not perform in battle as expected was explicable in terms of those very factors that Guderian had made known to Hitler in advance. This can be summed up by the simple observation that it was being sent into combat prematurely, months before it was finally declared by the Inspector General of Tank Troops to be 'combat ripe' – that is, free of the teething troubles that were to plague it at Kursk. The problems experienced are best illustrated by way of the figures for the daily availability of Panthers. On the opening seven days of the offensive – that is from 5 July though to 12 July – numbers fell from 184 serviceable machines to just 25!

OPPOSITE TOP Some days into the offensive, German air supremacy was no longer assured, and tank crews needed to camouflage their Panthers from Russian ground-attack aircraft using whatever brush was to hand.

OPPOSITE MIDDLE AND BOTTOM Two images wherein the tank commanders discuss the best way forward while their crews take a smoke break. Numbers of Panthers had dwindled alarmingly, such that by 10 July, only ten were operational.

Guderian himself had arrived on 10 July to see how his 'problem child' was doing and in his subsequent report to General Zeitzler, Head of the OKH, his breakdown of numbers of the non-operational machines over the period since the start of the offensive was as follows: with just 10 operational on the evening of that same day, of the 174 that had 'fallen out' since the 5th, 25 had been lost as 'total write-offs' (this includes the two that caught fire before the offensive began) to Soviet mines and anti-tank guns and dug-in T-34s; 100 were in need of repair, of which 56 had fallen out because of mines and enemy fire and 44 as a result of mechanical breakdown. He did note that of the broken-down machines 60% could be easily repaired; 40 had already been so and had been returned to service. He also observed that 25 had not yet been recovered but with just 4 turretless recovery Panthers available for the task, they were somewhat overwhelmed by demand. Alternative recovery methods required the use of three s.Zgkw. 18-ton half-tracks – the same number as needed to recover the Tiger I – but these were also in

ABOVE AND BELOW At the end of a day's combat the crews of these Panthers have turned the barrels through 90 degrees to permit them to be used as hangers for the strings of the *Zeltbahn* shelters. In the second image, the Panther in the background is already without its tracks and flying a pennant on its radio aerial signalling that it needs to be recovered.

heavy demand. Nor was there any low-loader in service that could handle the Panther, this leaving towing as the only means to evacuate damaged machines that could be repaired.

If 10 July marked the nadir of availability of operational Panthers, they saw an increase in the days thereafter as machines repaired by the Panzer *Werkstatt* were returned to service. Over the next week, through to 17 July, by which date offensive operations by 48th Panzer Corps had ground to a halt, the numbers rose and fell, with 44 operational on the final day of offensive operations. In short, some 25 Panthers were repaired and returned to service on a daily basis, but this number could have been raised had the spares situation been better. There was a great deal of cannibalisation of parts from knocked-out Panthers to compensate for the lack of spares. For example, in the case of the shortage of spare road wheels: '. . . With so many damages caused by mines, the road wheels are dismounted from every damaged Panther because they are urgently needed for the battle.'

It was reported that where Panthers had been destroyed by enemy fire from the 7.62cm

ABOVE Panther 245 is covered in dust – of a red hue – blending even more on the *Dunkelgelb* (dark yellow) and *Grün* (green) camouflage scheme the tank was painted in. One of the crew members is employing the tube on the side of the tank as a wedge to prevent himself slipping off as he tries to take a nap.

BELOW On the left of the image is a Panzer III which lies behind the Panther. The depressed barrel of the Panther on the right suggests that it has been knocked out. It is possible it wandered into a minefield.

ABOVE German officers stand and chat in front of a thoroughly cannibalised Panther. Gone is the muzzle brake, many of the road wheels and the tracks. In the light of the spares shortage, these parts were needed to keep other Panthers serviceable.

BELOW It was noted in the after-battle reports that the Panther was vulnerable to flank fire and this knocked-out example suggests that this is what happened here. There is a hole in the upper hull below the turret that seems to indicate that this Panther was caught by a Soviet 7.62cm anti-tank gun.

Soviet anti-tank gun or dug in T-34s firing the same calibre weapon, it had been brought about by the penetration of the sloping side armour on the hull and turret sides, even at ranges exceeding 1,000m. Such was reported by an Oberstleutnant Reinhold shortly after the end of the failed offensive. On 26 July he related that a high number of Panthers became unserviceable because of hits to the side

armour which was easily penetrated. He stated that 'for that reason there were very frequent write-offs because the vehicle burns out due to ammunition or fuel igniting'.

A year later, Guderian would once again be reporting on the frequency of this occurrence from the 'Invasion Front' in Normandy. However, in all cases, the armour of the glacis had not been defeated, with not one Panther being lost to penetrations of it. Notwithstanding Hitler's concern that 80mm of frontal armour would not be adequate to cope with up-rated Russian and other anti-tank weapons in 1943, the thickness proved generally effective through to 1945. However, by then, the appearance of much heavier weaponry (such as the Soviet BS-3 100m anti-tank gun and 122mm and 152mm weapons on the Red Army JS-II and ISU-122 and 152, the British 17pdr anti-tank gun also mounted on lend-lease M4s and the same modified weapon on the Comet medium tank) would have seen the Panther becoming increasingly vulnerable had the war continued. It was, however, the problem with the weaker flank hull armour that prompted Guderian to assert that: 'Close attention must be paid to guarding the flanks of the Panther attack! All other weapons must be employed in this effort!'

This issue was compounded of course by the almost complete lack of training time prior to the battle, but it took the Panther's first foray into combat to make the point. Although penned after Kursk, the following takes account of what had to be done to protect the Panther as a primary combat asset:

It is particularly important to ensure flank protection for the 'sensitive' sides of the Panther tanks. The Pz.Rgt commander must always keep a reserve up his sleeve, which he can use at a moment's notice to block any threat from the flank. . . . This reserve should normally be about 1100 yards in the rear. It has been found advisable to let the available Mark IVs in the Pz.Rgt take over the task of protection from the flanks, while the Panthers quickly press on and drive a wedge into the enemy position.

But even as early as Kursk it was noted that shells which hit the gun mantlet could ricochet downwards and go through the roof, causing the driver and the radio operator to become casualties. It was also noted, however, that to do anything to counter this by reinforcing the armour would only overstress the suspension, and that the Panther could not take any heavier weight.

From Kursk through to the early spring of 1944, the only theatre in which the Panther saw action was in Russia. The bulk of Panther Ausf D production was sent to Russia and were lost in that theatre with only a small number surviving to see action in Italy in 1944. However, on 22 February 1944, Guderian was able to report that in his opinion the Panther could no longer be viewed as a 'problem child'. Although not all difficulties with the type had been eliminated (and never would be) the most persistent and significant had been eradicated. Therefore, he was able to report:

In its present form the Panther is troop ripe. It is far superior to the T-34 tank. Almost all the bugs have been worked out. This Panzer has exceptional armament, armour, cross-country travel ability and speed. At this time the lifespan of the motor is 700 to 1,000 kilometres. Motor failures have decreased. Final drive breakdowns no longer occur. The steering gear and transmissions have proven to be acceptable.

BELOW Where Panthers could not be recovered they were, if time and conditions permitted, blown up.

RIGHT Panthers were involved in the heavy fighting that saw the retreat of the German Army after Kursk. This is an early version of an Ausf A that still has the letterbox flap for the machine gun in the glacis.

Aspects of this report are somewhat over-optimistic. It was not the case that the final drive breakdowns no longer occurred – they did and this facet of the tank was to cause problems through to the end of the war. Evidence for this can be found in the report on I/Pz.Rgt 4 cited on page 133.

The Panther in action post-Kursk

With the close of 1943, the German forces in southern Russia had been pushed back by the Red Army to beyond the river Dnieper. By this date, the Panther had been in service for six months with both the Army and the Waffen SS, with no fewer than 841 of 1,768 produced in 1943 having been despatched eastward to serve in the Panther *Abteilungen.* Of those that had been raised and were being raised in Germany, nine had been despatched and were in service on the Eastern Front, primarily in southern Russia, by the end of the year. They are detailed in Table 1 below.

Losses, however, had been high with no fewer than 624 having been written off in that period, with on average barely 100 Panthers

TABLE 1			
Panzer *Abteilung* **(Pz.Abt)**	**Number of Panthers allocated to the unit**	**Date arrived at the front (all 1943)**	**Unit the Pz.Abt was attached to**
Pz.Abt 51	96	1 July	*GD* PzGr. Div
Pz.Abt 52	96	4 July	*GD* PzGr. Div
I/SS. Pz.Abt 25	71	22 August	I SS PzGr. Div
I/Pz.Abt 15 (redesignated Pz.Abt 52)	96	24 August	11 Pz.Div
II/ Pz.Abt 23	96	31 August	23 Pz.Div
1/Pz.Abt 2	71	2 October	13 Pz.Div
I/SS. Pz.Abt 1	96	9 November	I SS Pz.Div LAH
1/Pz.Abt 1	76	11 November	1 Pz.Div
I/Pz.Abt 31	76	5 December	To XI. Corps 15 December, and to 3rd Pz. Corps on 27 December

TABLE 2					
July	**August**	**September**	**October**	**November**	**December**
173	21	63	71	112	Not given

operational per month. The potential of the Panther continued to be hamstrung by the still large number of technical problems associated with the design and many were with the *Werkstatt* units awaiting repair. But such was the tempo of operations post-Kursk that many had to be abandoned in the westward retreat as there were not enough recovery machines or tank transporters available. Even these also became victims and when there was time for the *Werkstatt* units to get to grips with the problems on the Panther, there was an ongoing difficulty with the supply of spare parts. These factors are reflected in the numbers of Panthers repaired in the period July–December 1943 and detailed in Table 2 opposite.

It was normally the case that severely damaged tanks of all types were returned to Germany for extensive repair or rebuild. But even here problems were being experienced in the homeland that severely impacted upon the provision of this facility. For example, in November, just 20 Panthers were returned to Germany for repair. When in early 1944, Hitler insisted that far more damaged machines be returned to the homeland for repair (this included all types of panzers and other AFVs, not just Panthers) a representative of the Ministry for Armaments and War Production observed that 'Panzer maintenance in the homeland is ending in disaster' as the *Heimatinstandsetzung* that was responsible for carrying this out, 'was quite simply unable to process the evacuated panzers'.

It was not that the Red Army had dealt out heavy losses on the German medium tank; indeed the number attributed to the guns of the T-34 were far fewer than the total number of Panthers lost. The withdrawal of the German Army westward after Kursk had led to the abandonment of many disabled Panthers that would have otherwise been recovered and repaired. Strength returns as of 31 December 1943 revealed that 217 Panthers were available, but of these just 80 were operational. The differential is indicative of the very high drop-out rate due to technical failings as well as combat damage.

It was only in the new year of 1944 that the Panther was to see combat in theatres other than the Soviet Union, initially in Italy and later in the year in northern France, in Normandy.

The Panther in Italy

Although the Allies invaded Sicily in July, and then mainland Italy in September 1943, their encounter with German armoured units found them pitting their M4s and Churchills primarily against German Mark IIIs, IVs and StuG IIIs. The Panther was first met with the arrival of I/Pz.Rgt 4, which had 76 Panthers on strength in early 1944. This was the only formation to employ this panzer to serve in Italy, remaining there until the German surrender in 1945. At no time during its service there did the total number of Panthers on strength exceed the number brought with them from France. Replacements were delivered on a sporadic basis, but Italy was a theatre of war that was deemed of less significance than the Eastern Front and also from January 1944 onwards, France, as units there were 'beefed-up' on the assumption that Allied landings would take place during the course of the summer. I/Pz.Rgt 4 retained its identity until it was subsumed into 26th Pz.Div on 16 February 1945, whereupon it was redesignated 1./26.

I/Pz.Rgt 4 found itself serving alongside s.Pz.Abt (Sturmpanzer Abteilung) 216 with 57 Sturmpanzer IVs, s.Pz.Abt 508 with 45 Tiger Is, Pz.Abt(fkl) 301 with 30 StuG IIIs and 11 Elefants (formerly Ferdinand *schwere PanzerJäger*) of s.Pz.Jg.Abt 653 – all under the auspices of Pz.Rgt 69. The deployment of these units was a response to the Allied landings on 22 January 1944 at Anzio, at the time many miles behind the then front line to the south and theoretically within striking distance of Rome. Although on paper a most formidable assemblage of heavy armour (and this included the Panther), this formation was hampered by Italy's undulating and mountainous terrain. There is no equivalent to the steppe such that the Panther could take advantage of the long range of its gun. The country is generally hilly, the roads are winding (and in many cases narrow) and there are frequent sections that are steep, which placed great strain on the drivetrains and transmissions. Quite often the mileage accrued by a Panther when traversing the sort of mountainous terrain found in Italy – the Alps to the north and the Apennines running down the spine of the peninsula – contributed to

Panther Ausf Ds of I/Pz.Rgt 4 are seen with a Borgward tracked remote-controlled demolition vehicle of a *Funklenk* unit (a radio-controlled demolition unit) on one of the main roads leading to the Anzio Front. The StuG III in the second image and in front of the line of Panthers is the control vehicle for the Borgward.

reducing the life of the engine and transmission. Nor did the fields, with their hedges and trees, permit the main gun to be gainfully employed. Furthermore, for the first time, they experienced the overwhelming superiority of Allied air power and its ability to severely limit the capacity of panzer units to execute ground operations.

Having made passage through Rome in February, I/Pz.Rgt 4 was directed towards the Anzio–Nettuno bridgehead, where it was assembled with the other elements of Pz.Rgt 69.

Although there were a few early Ausf Ds, most of the Panthers were early Ausf As that could be identified by the new cast cupola fitted in place of the original drum type. I/Pz.Rgt 4 was committed to combat on 16 February with the launch of the German offensive against the Anzio bridgehead in conditions hardly suitable either for the Panther or the other heavier machines.

The battle raged for four days under lowering skies and over open waterlogged country

with miles of wire, minefields, weapon pits and trenches and with shell holes and scrapes everywhere, so that the German diarist was to record that the conditions for the first time anywhere did approach that of the First World War.

For the Panther, as well as the Tiger and Elefant, the conditions were such that it was rarely possible for them to depart from the roads, for to do so would see them succumb

to the mud and other traps of the battlefield. Hitler's intention in despatching these valuable combat units to this front was predicated on his conviction that – as at Kursk – they must inevitably break through the Allied defences. He exercised total control of the operation from his HQ in East Prussia, dictating both the direction and, once begun, the course of the whole offensive. It failed. For I/Pz.Rgt 4 the experience was not a good one. Losses, albeit light, nonetheless resulted in the unnecessary

ABOVE A row of Panthers line the same road as in the previous image. The problem for the Panther, as for the Tiger Is and the Elefants which had also been despatched by Hitler to liquidate the Allied forces at Anzio, was the extremely muddy conditions that were found off-road.

LEFT A Panzerbefehlswagen Panther along the same main road facing the Allied bridgehead while in front lies a knocked-out Elefant heavy *PanzerJäger*.

writing-off of valuable machines that could have been better employed elsewhere. It was, however, further to the south, around Monte Cassino, that the Panthers would face their first encounters with British and US armour.

At Anzio the British and US Armies had their first encounters with the Panther. Until its appearance in Italy, the only information about this new German medium tank had come via the Russians who forwarded intelligence with photographs of captured examples. An actual

Panther that fought with Pz.Abt 51 at Kursk, built by MAN in late May/early June 1943, was shipped to the UK. In May 1944, elements of I/Pz.Rgt 4 were involved in the fighting to try to stop the Allied advance following the fall of Monte Cassino. The Allied offensive began on 22 May and the war diary of the 4th Company of Pz.Rgt 4 described how the unit found itself attempting to hold back the enemy advance. The formation was alerted at 03.55 hours the next day. Just under an hour later three

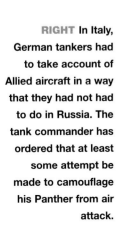

Panthers left the assembly area with four others due to follow once they had refuelled. This was a prolonged process as there was only one hand pump to transfer the fuel from 200-litre drums and even as this was being completed, at 05.15 Allied artillery started with a heavy barrage forcing the panzers to shift position.

Enemy tanks [M4s] and infantry started to attack at 10.30. A decision was made to attack the enemy in the flank. The route was subjected to heavy artillery barrages. Finding the way was almost impossible because of the powder fumes and artificial smoke. Bypassing the various barrage zones, five Panthers managed to attack the enemy in the flank without loss due to enemy fire. Panthers 423 and 431 had remained behind due to mechanical problems. The opponent fled the battlefield, pulling back to the east, leaving all his weapons and equipment behind. An immediate enemy tank counter-attack was repulsed. Panther 433 was knocked out in the last action. The commander was killed and the gunner and loader wounded. A short time later the gunner in Panther 423 was wounded.

All of the enemy tank attacks were beaten back. Altogether 28 enemy tanks were destroyed. Nine were claimed by

Panther 433, six by Panther 422, five each by Panthers 415 and 414 and three by 401. All 28 of these enemy tanks burned immediately. Three additional tanks were knocked out but didn't burn and were not claimed as kills.

The war diary added a few days later:

During the combat on 23 and 24 May 1944, the company lost six Panthers as total write-offs

ABOVE A Zimmerit-covered, solid sand yellow-painted early Ausf A, sporting a very different type of camouflage on the gun barrel.

LEFT A rather more graphic image to illustrate the steps taken by this tank crew to protect their Panther both from the air and the ground.

Inasmuch as the designers of the Panther understood that their creation had been, in the first instance, designed to deal with the T-34, the combat debut of the German medium tank at Kursk demonstrated conclusively that its main armament of the 75mm L/70 had satisfied that primary requirement. Though the battle was lost, the number of T-34s destroyed by the Panther was high, with the Red Army losing a far greater number of tanks to the Germans in realising victory. Even Stalin was forced to accept that depending on the mass production of the 76.2mm model of the T-34 could no longer be maintained when it was clear that any of the residual superiority of the T-34 had now disappeared. For Soviet tankers the new reality was that: 'the arrival of the Panther and

the Tiger tanks turned the tables. . . . Their long guns allowed them to fight without bothering about concealment. . . . Based on the fact that our 76mm guns could only pierce their armour from 500 metres they stood out in the open.'

Even the special tungsten-cored ammunition carried in small numbers on each T-34, was no longer adequate to the task.

The Red Army had thus found itself in a situation from the very outset of its encounter with the Panther that would be duplicated with the British and US Armies a year hence in Normandy. That is, that their tanks were under-gunned. Stalin therefore sanctioned the up-gunning of the T-34 to allow it to cope with the Panther and the Tiger.

It took until the early spring of 1944

BELOW Working captured Panthers, as with other captured German tanks, were pressed into the Red Army and used until they broke down. Note the large white stars on the turrets. *(Author)*

for this new model of the T-34 to emerge. Equipped with a new three-man turret and a commander's cupola that did much to enhance its effectiveness, it mounted an 85mm gun; while it was not as valuable as the 75mm gun of the Panther it nonetheless did much to raise the capability of the Red Army's tank army. What is more, it had the advantage of being produced in huge numbers. Whereas the three companies building the Panther Ausf G (which went into production at more or less the same time in Germany as the T-34/85 went into service with the Red Army) produced 2,650 Panthers by war's end, the numerous factories mass-producing the T-34/85 had manufactured 14,648 of this new model by the end of 1944! It is such a statistic that made the notion that the

Panther could secure 'combat dominance' on the battlefields in the East so illusory.

Russian tankers were greatly enthused with their new charge, but it was not just the T-34 that was doing much to enhance the performance of the Soviet Tank Arm. The IS-II heavy tank, although at 44 tons almost the same weight as the Panther medium tank, mounted a 122mm gun. It was able to stand off and shoot at the Panther at some distance and destroy it. The problem for the Panther was also magnified by the gamut of self-propelled guns introduced by the Red Army between 1944 and 1945. Based on the T-34 chassis, first came the SU-85, which was replaced by the more powerful SU-100. On the IS-II chassis came the ISU-122 and ISU-152. These filled roles analogous to the German assault guns and *PanzerJäger*.

For T-34 tankers, even if armed with an 85mm weapon, it remained the case that they were taught to stalk their German prey and hit the Panther in its more vulnerable flanks. With the 85mm gun it was still not possible to assure a penetration of the Panther's frontal glacis armour and losses continued to be high in consequence of factors including superior German training.

However, even in January 1945 German tankers were writing in the post-battle reports that:

> the anti-tank guns are the main [author's emphasis] opponents of Panzers in the Eastern Theatre of war. The Russians use anti-tank guns en masse for defence or by cleverly towing them along behind an attack to swiftly bring them into action . . . these weapons are concentrated as PaKnests in an attempt to achieve long-range flank firing.

The Red Army deployed thousands of anti-tank guns in their major operations and as the war went on, the calibre of their anti-tank weapons also increased, culminating in the 100mm BS-3, which went into service in 1944. By the end of the conflict, the Panther, although still effective, was not regarded by the Red Army with the trepidation it had felt in 1943. They had taken the measure of the beast.

RIGHT This early Panther Ausf A wears a complete coating of Zimmerit, some of which has already come away from the front of the two track guards. The Panther is in travelling mode as the gun barrel is locked in the travel bracket.

in exchange for destroying a total of 33 enemy tanks. Five Panthers (401, 411, 414, 415 and 422) burned out due to fire from enemy tanks. After running out of fuel, and already damaged by hits from enemy tank fire, Panther 433 burned out when hit by artillery fire.

In consequence of the offensive the Allies captured Rome on 6 June. In the light of the losses of Panthers, a further 38 were shipped from the Army Ordnance depot in Germany as replacements between 27 May and 4 June. As in Russia, the losses of Panthers relative to those of British and American tanks were always much lower but the Germans were facing the ongoing problem that could never be resolved: that they could never hope to defeat the far greater number of machines pouring out of the tank factories in the USA, the UK and the Soviet Union.

I/Pz.Rgt 4 thereafter found itself withdrawing northward as the Germans retreated, into northern Italy, perforce abandoning Panthers that had broken down or been lost to enemy fire. They received their final batch of 20 replacement Panthers between 18 and 21 September 1944. By 1 April 1945, the by then redesignated Panther Regiment of 26th Pz.Div had been reduced to just 25 machines,

of which 22 were operational. Those still surviving at the time of the German surrender were handed over to the Allies.

Panthers in action on the eastern border of Poland, late summer 1944

The summer of 1944 saw the German Army experience the greatest defeat in its history. Operation Bagration – the Red Army's summer offensive – destroyed Army Group Centre and drove the surviving German forces in Belorussia back to the Russo-Polish border. Launched on 22 June – three years after the Germans attacked the Soviet Union – it caught the bulk of the German Army's mobile formations to the south in Ukraine, where it had been assumed the Red Army would strike.

By July 1944, the Red Army had reached the borders of Poland and was in striking distance of the capital city of Warsaw. It was here that the German Army and the *Panzerwaffe* achieved one of its very last tactical victories in a large tank battle at Macieyov. It was, however, a purely defensive success and one that at best provided a local hiatus in the westward advance of the Red Army. It was also a battle that was

LEFT The heavy tank battles in the late summer of 1944 on the Eastern Front brought a few local victories for the *Panzerwaffe*, of which much was made of by the cameramen of the Propaganda Kompanie. A Panther commander sweeps the horizon for approaching Soviet armour.

BELOW A Panther Ausf A constructed after August 1944. It gives the appearance of being an almost brand-new machine recently delivered to the front.

ABOVE **Although not on a par with that of the Normandy Front, it was nonetheless the case that the Red Air Force was increasingly coming to dominate the skies in the East. Here Panthers, and on the right the side of a *Möbelwagen* anti-aircraft tank, can be seen taking cover in a wood.**

covered extremely well by the cameramen of the Propaganda Kompanie. From our point of view, the film and stills derived from it show the Panther operating in the optimum combat conditions for which it was originally designed – the flat, steppe-like lands of eastern Poland.

After the collapse of Army Group Centre, Hitler had passed the command of its remnants to Field Marshal Walter Model. This, in addition to his command of Army Group North Ukraine, meant that he could co-ordinate the few surviving forces in order to create defensive deployments to the east of Warsaw. By 28 July Lieutenant General A.F. Popov's 8th Guards Tank Corps had fought its way to within 20km of Warsaw when its lead formation, Major General N.D. Vedennev's 3rd Tank Corps, plunged headlong into a succession of counter-attacks by panzer formations deployed for that purpose by Model. On 30 July, the initial counter-attack was launched by the Hermann Goering Pz.Div and the 19th Pz.Div some 15km to the north-east of Warsaw. On 2 and

3 August, 4th Pz.Div and the 4 SS Pz.Div *Wiking* were added to the mix. It is at this point, and in particular with the involvement of *Wiking*, that we shall focus.

The latter formation had spent the time since its battle at Kovel earlier in the year rebuilding. It had been partially re-formed by 1 June when it reported having 77 Panthers and 73 Panzer IVs on strength (the bulk of the latter non-operational).

Between 3 and 7 August elements of *Wiking* and elements of 3rd SS Pz.Div *Totenkopf* were involved in heavy tank fights in the fields outside Praga with the Soviet 3rd Tank Corps of 2nd Tank Army. In a rolling series of encounters along a front before Warsaw, components of these two German formations found themselves defending a stretch of the front between Mińsk-Mazowiecki and Kałuszyn. It was on 2 August that they found themselves on the defensive against assaults by 8th Tank Guards Corps supported by 47th Army's most advanced units. It was here, in the author's opinion, that the film was shot that was later shown on the *Deutsche Wochenschau* in German cinemas a week later.

The Panthers of *Wiking*'s battalion were seen advancing across rolling fields of ripening wheat and periodically stopping to fire at

distant targets. The movie footage and stills suggest that the weather was good and visibility excellent. These were the conditions for which the Panther was designed to operate at its best. The Panthers are seen to advance across the open fields, supported by infantry moving through the wheat, stopping every so often to fire on a target ahead. It is worth noting that there is no concern on the part of the SS tankers with enemy aircraft – they are noticeable by their absence – something that their comrades fighting at the same time in Normandy simply could not do. Indeed, an advance such as this in Normandy would have been unthinkable at this time. Nor are the attacking Germans supported by flak vehicles. The sequence ends with the coverage of destroyed T-34/85s and a small number

ABOVE Command staff of SS *Wiking* use both a Sd.Kfz. 251/3 and a Panzerbefehlswagen Panther to co-ordinate and control the deployment of their forces.

LEFT A Panzerbefehlswagen Panther Ausf G wearing a dark yellow and green camouflage finish advances through the rolling wheat fields towards the Russian positions. It has the full panoply of aerials on the turret and rear hull.

RIGHT An
SS *Wiking* Panther
Ausf G numbered 411
moves forward with
supporting infantry
towards the enemy.

BELOW A Panther
Ausf G powers down
a dusty track followed
by an Sd.Kfz. 251
armoured personnel
carrier.

of IS-II tanks. The latter was more frequently encountered, having gone into service only in early 1944. The German claims for the number of Russian tanks destroyed in this and the wider operations around Warsaw in the following days totalled over 400.

The inclusion of the images to support this section, most if not all taken from the film

footage as stills, give an excellent impression of Panther operations towards the end of the summer of 1944 on the Eastern Front. The simple fact was that although the Panther was crucial in helping to inflict localised victories on the advancing Red Army, the strategic situation was such that they were at best very temporary brakes on the continuing westward advance of Stalin's army.

A similar localised tactical victory that inflicted significant losses on the Red Army had taken place a few months before the clash described above. The *Grossdeutschland* (GD) tank division, under the command of Lieutenant General Hasso von Manteuffel, had inflicted an earlier defeat on the Red Army at Târgu Frumos in Rumania in early May 1944. With a force of 22 Panzer IVs, 6 to 7 Tigers and between 8 and 10 Panthers, the German forces claimed to have destroyed more than 200 Russian tanks. At the same time the GD division, which had been

formed only the year before, claimed its 1,000th enemy tank destroyed, of which its Panther battalion was responsible for a high number.

Von Manteuffel penned a report following the Târgu Frumos encounter, which crystallised his thoughts on Panzer operations and as such represent the essence of German tank tactics in the summer of 1944 and through to the end of the war. They applied to any tank formation serving in the *Panzerwaffe*, irrespective of tank type. However, of particular note is the degree to which what is contained herein could not have been achieved in the very different combat environment of Normandy. In the East, the Panther could still be a Panther, but in Normandy this cat was severely restricted in how it could fight – as we shall see:

BELOW A quick discussion as to what to do. The Panther is replete with a full coat of Zimmerit and carries an anti-aircraft mount on the cupola ring.

ABOVE The same Sd.Kfz. 251 and Panzerbefehlswagen Panther seen earlier, but from a different perspective. These two machines belong to SS *Wiking*.

In an armoured battle, all other branches must be subordinated to support our tanks, unconditionally.

The tanks should not be content with defending against attacking enemy tanks from good shooting positions, but destroying them wherever they see them or guess where they are. For this reason, tanks must always attack again and again.

Movement and fire are to be combined, even in a tank-versus-tank battle, in order to prevent oneself from being attacked.

Only deploy as many tanks in defence as are needed to master the situation. The tank battle must develop from behind, and at all times one must have a battle-ready reserve of tanks, particularly those with heavier guns, eg the Panther and Tiger.

The speed of the tank on the battlefield, not that on the road, has proved, along with good leadership and shooting skills of

RIGHT A Panther Ausf A moves through a small town in Holland. The image shows to good effect the hangers on which the *Schürzen* side panels were hung, albeit only one is to be seen on this side of the panzer.

the crews, to be a decisive pre-condition for a successful engagement against enemy tanks.

Tank commanders up to the divisional commander belong on the field of battle and indeed wherever the seat of the fight can be found.

Von Manteuffel would apply these insights right through to the Ardennes offensive at the end of December 1944. However, the onset of the Allied invasion on 6 June 1944 found the Panther-equipped units having to fight in conditions that were the antithesis of that set down by von Manteuffel.

Preparing for the invasion in the West

Hitler had expressed his intention at the end of 1943 to see a priority given to the build-up in the strength of German armoured forces in the West, on the presumption that an Allied invasion of the continent of Europe could be expected in the summer of 1944. Between January and June 1944, a further five Panther battalions were raised in Germany with at least four having 79 Panthers on strength.

A number of these went to increase the number of Panthers available in the West. These showed a steady rise from 157 in

December 1943, to 290 in February 1944 and 514 in April with a high of 655 reached by 10 June. That the West was receiving priority in the delivery of Panthers is indicated by the number serving in Russia at the end of May 1944, where there were just 313 on strength – this being a date before the start of Operation Bagration – the massive Soviet summer offensive.

Panthers in Normandy

The German ability to defeat the expected Allied landing(s) was in the first instance hamstrung by their uncertainty as to where these would take place. Both Hitler and Rommel eventually settled on the view that Normandy was most likely, but as an initial landing place, so as to draw off German formations from the presumed main landing site on the Pas de Calais. Neither the Germans nor the Allies were in any doubt that the primary instrument to be employed to effect the destruction of the Allied landings would be the panzer divisions. Indeed Rommel, commander of Army Group B, was vehement in his conviction that the invasion had to be defeated on the beaches, and in the first 24 hours.

But of course, in the absence of the intelligence needed to deploy them in very close proximity to where the landings would actually take place, this could not hope to be realised. Neither did Rommel have a free hand in the deployment of the panzer divisions, nor in the numbers under his control. There was disagreement between Rommel and Leo Geyr von Schweppenburg – the commander of *Panzergruppe* West – who wished to hold back the bulk of the armoured divisions for a massive counter strike once the 'fog of war' had cleared and the Germans knew where the main landings were taking place. Rommel ridiculed this notion, as such a massed attack would be defeated by the Allies' massive air power, something that von Schweppenburg, having served his time on the Eastern Front, had never experienced. To resolve the matter, Hitler had stepped in on 26 April and resolved the *Panzerkontroversie* by imposing a solution that satisfied neither man. Rommel was allocated three panzer divisions – the 2nd, the 21st and the 116th – but he was not free to decide their deployment, being dispersed from Normandy through to Amiens. Von Schweppenburg saw his command reduced to four divisions, namely the 12th SS Panzer, *Panzer Lehr*, 17th SS Panzer Grenadier and I SS Panzer Division. These, however, would require Hitler's permission before they could be released for action. The remainder, II SS, 9th Panzer and 11th Panzer were allocated to Army Group G in southern France.

This being the case, neither man had the necessary forces to realise either of their respective plans. On 6 June 1944, the number of Panthers deployed in France meant that it was the second most numerous tank in the theatre after the Panzer IV. However, not all of the Panzer Divisions were fielding Panthers. Neither the 11th Pz.Div, 21st Pz.Div or the 116th Pz.Div had any on strength.

On 10 June, General Heinz Guderian, acting in his capacity of Inspector General of Panzer Troops, submitted a report to Hitler on tank strength in the theatre. The number of Panthers serving in divisions is shown in the table below.

Panzer Lehr	2.Pz.Div	9.Pz.Div	I SS Pz.Div	II SS Pz.Div	12 SS Pz.Div
88	79	40	54	78	66

Those listed below were, on 10 June, still rebuilding.

1.Pz.Rgt 15	1.Pz.Rgt 24	1.Pz.Rgt 25	1.Pz.Rgt 27	1.Pz.Rgt 29	1.Pz.Rgt 36	1.Pz.Rgt GD*	I SS Pz.Rgt 3	I SS Pz.Rgt 9	I SS Pz.Rgt 10
4	9	11	79	8	10	79	6	40	4

* Sent to Lithuania on 10 July and placed under command of 6.Pz.Div.

LEFT A Panther Ausf A moves at speed down a narrow road on the Normandy Front. It did not take very long after the invasion on 6 June for movement in daylight, as seen in the picture, to effectively mean dicing with death given the overwhelming presence of Allied air power.

The Allied troops' first encounter with the Panther came within a few days of the landings. Both the 12th SS Panzer and *Panzer Lehr* found themselves engaged in heavy fighting with British and Canadian troops to the west of the city of Caen, which had been targeted for capture on the day of the invasion. Indeed, so great was the importance of this city to both sides, that prevention of its capture 'drew German armoured formations' to its defence such that by mid-June the bulk of the panzer divisions were engaged there. US forces on the Cotentin Peninsula did not find themselves having to contend with the Panther until *Panzer Lehr* was redeployed to the St Lô–Coutances area on 2 July.

It was only on the afternoon of 7 July that the commander of *Panzer Lehr* reached the front, but his division was still stretched out along its march route. Indeed, the Panthers of this division were, on 6 June, being entrained for transport to Poland although this was cancelled by General Bayerlein, the divisional commander. It then took until 10 June for the

BELOW The close country and narrow lanes that formed the bulk of the countryside in Normandy was not ideal terrain in which the Panther could fight. This image well conveys what a big machine it was.

ABOVE AND RIGHT These two images illustrate a Panzerbefehlswagen Panther wearing the number 96 on the rear of the turret. It is an Ausf A. The turret sides are festooned with extra track links added by the tank crew as, in this close country, infantry with anti-tank weapons such as the British PIAT (projectile infantry anti-tank) – although cumbersome – was effective at close quarters.

Panthers to join with the rest of the division at the front. Nor would the armour of the 12th SS be available to help effect the concentration of armour for the planned counter-attack by I SS Pz.Corps, the reason being that 'tanks of both divisions had to cover very long distances – for the most part on paved roads – and needed to halt for repairs and refuelling'. In fact, the 48 combat-ready Panthers of I SS Pz.Bn of 12th SS Pz.Div had run out of fuel to the east of the river Orne. Even so, the corps commander Sepp Dietrich ordered the counter-attack for the morning of the following day, employing the armour of both divisions.

This counter-attack did not come to fruition for the same reason that all others the Germans planned for in the Normandy operation did not either. Forewarned by ENIGMA intercepts of any concentration of German armour, this was targeted by the British and Canadians with mass artillery fire, very heavy naval gunfire and aerial bombardment. German armour found itself tied down to defending against a succession of British and Canadian offensive drives through the bocage (mixed woodland and pasture terrain) to the west of Caen, wherein, according to Guderian in a report to Hitler: 'The main pressure from enemy tanks in tank-unfavourable country lay – as expected – on streets and lanes. This is where the main battles took place.'

In such an environment the main armament of both the Panther and Tiger was severely constrained and their advantage in terms of gun power significantly reduced.

The slowness of the arrival of German reinforcements saw armoured divisions fed into the line in dribs and drabs to make up for machines that had either been destroyed or fallen out because of technical problems. They were thus never able to concentrate sufficient force to launch any significant operation that could seriously endanger the Allied lodgement.

General Marcks, one of the original authors of the Barbarossa plan mentioned in Chapter 1, stated the day before his death in Normandy, that 10 June was the last day on which the invasion could have been defeated. The German armoured force in Normandy was slowly reduced by a process of attrition in the face of an Allied force growing ever stronger

on a daily basis. Rommel stated as much in a report to the OKW (Oberkommando der Wehrmacht) on 12 June:

Our operations in Normandy are . . . rendered extremely difficult, and in part impossible to carry out, by the following factors: the extremely strong and in some respects overwhelming superiority of the enemy air force . . . the enemy had complete command of the air over the battle up to about 100km behind the front and cuts off by day . . . almost all traffic on roads or by roads or in open country. Movement of our troops on the field of battle by day are thus almost entirely prevented, while the enemy can operate freely.

In consequence of the effectiveness of Allied air power, it was ordered that movements of panzers should only take place at night between 22.30 and 05.30 hours. Drivers were instructed never to use their lights. Unsurprisingly, the order was issued that 'all panzers will be camouflaged. Flat surfaces

BELOW Three members of the crew of the Panther Ausf G behind them, stand away from their charge in earnest discussion. It is a reasonable inference to draw that their tank has broken down as leaving it in the open was an invitation to any passing Allied *Jabo* to pounce. Note that it carries two spare road wheels attached to the turret and that the circular tube carrying the gun-cleaning rods is here mounted across the rear of the hull.

75mm L70

German infantry inch forward down a narrow lane covered by the Panther bringing up the rear. It is worth noting the height of the hedgerows against the size of the Panther. PIAT (projectile infantry anti-tank) – although cumbersome – was effective at close quarters.

will be covered with wire netting on which foliage will be interlaced. The *Schürzen* will be camouflaged in this manner.' In addition, it was Guderian, in his capacity of Inspector General of Tank Troops, who issued the strict admonition on the use of radios:

> In all cases [author's emphasis] forbid the use of radio communication even for tuning in. This applies to assembly areas. Several times units behind the front were covered by carpet bombing after sending a few radio messages.

The Panther – 'feared and respected'

That being said, Allied armour was over the course of the campaign to pay a high price for its ultimate victory in Normandy and there is no question that the Panther played a major role in inflicting the losses that were experienced. At the time of the invasion 'the Panther was something of an unknown quantity, certainly to British tank crews, who were extremely unlikely to have encountered them before Overlord'. Although one had been received from the Russians and a number had fallen into the hands of the Allies in Italy,

the latter had happened too late for any real intelligence on the machine to reach units to be sent to France.

Once ashore and moving inland, however, this German panzer very quickly made an impression on the British and Canadian tank crews who became acquainted with its formidable armament and frontal armour. It was quickly ascertained that the Panther's 75mm L/70 high-velocity main armament had the ability to penetrate the armour of any Allied tank at battle ranges, even the very heavily armoured Churchill, where armour thickness of the latest mark in service was 152mm. The accompanying diagram graphically illustrates the disadvantage that the M4 – the most numerous Allied tank in Normandy – had, along with the British Cromwell and Churchill in terms of gun power when facing the Panther.

Notwithstanding the reputation of the Tiger I heavy tank, it was the expressed view of a number of British tank commanders and senior officers that it was the Panther that was 'feared and respected by Allied tank crews, more so than any other German tank' and indeed proved to be the greatest problem. 'British tank crews quickly recognised that the fast-moving and manoeuvrable Panther was a formidable opponent in all circumstances and situations.'

BELOW A diagram that shows the difficulties Allied armour laboured under in seeking to combat the Panther. In all cases with three tanks shown here, the M4 (top on right), Cromwell and Churchill (bottom) were all equipped with the same medium-velocity 75mm gun. All were out-ranged by the Panther.

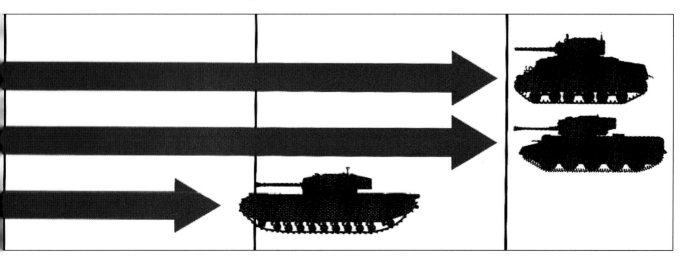

BELOW Panther 438 is wearing full Zimmerit – it is an Ausf A with the triple exhaust on the rear of the hull. The long length of the 75mm L/70 main gun is well illustrated here – it straddles the whole width of the road.

In a report to his superior, Brigadier H. Pyman stated that: 'The result is while the 75mm shot [of the Allies] has been failing to penetrate the front face of the Tiger and Panthers at ranges down to 30 yards, they can knock Shermans [M4] and Cromwells out at ranges up to 1,500 yards with ease.'

The only tank possessed by the Allies that could take on a Panther (and Tiger) at battle ranges was a British conversion of the M4 called the 'Firefly'. Armed with a 17pdr anti-tank gun at the time of the invasion, it was only available in limited numbers, but these

increased as the campaign went on. The M4 was the standard tank of most armoured and independent tank brigades in Normandy and in the tank troops (each of four tanks), one would be a Firefly. The weapon also equipped the lend-lease-supplied M10 wherein the normal 3in main gun was replaced by the 17pdr and was rechristened as the Achilles. However, its standard APCBA (armour-piercing capped ballistic cap) had difficulties penetrating the frontal armour of the Panther at battle ranges. The newer APDS (armour-piercing discarding sabot) round was more effective, having

a higher muzzle velocity, but 'the fall off in accuracy proved to be a minor inconvenience in the close terrain of Normandy'. The following short account from the war diary of the British 29th Armoured Brigade for 27 June illustrates the impact of the Firefly in fights with Panthers – although it is clear that not all of the British tanks involved were armed with the 17pdr:

> *The first encounter took place in the early morning. At 07.50, three Panthers were engaged, with one being destroyed before the others withdrew. Half an hour later, they*

and elements of 8th Armoured Brigade engaged five Panthers, knocking out four with only one escaping.

The Germans understandably rapidly identified the Firefly as being the priority target, such that it was advised that troop leaders not use one as their command tank.

To defeat the Germans in Normandy, the British Army had no choice but to attack through the bocage, to the west of Caen, in most cases frontally, and this played to the weaknesses of Allied armour in both their too-

BELOW On *Jabo* watch – a crewman sits atop the turret and, with the commander in the Panther's cupola, they scan the sky for any appearance of the dreaded Allied fighter-bombers. It is for that reason that the crew has taken especial care to fix foliage to their tank.

thin frontal armour in the case of the most numerous Allied tank – the M4 – and the almost uniform use of the US 75mm medium-velocity (MV) main armament employed on the M4, the Cromwell and Churchill tanks. Major Bill Close of the 11th Armoured Division later wrote about how the terrain – that is the bocage – that his men's tanks had to drive through was to the advantage of the German defenders.

Bocage was different entirely; it's not good tank country. We found it most difficult to operate in the bocage . . . very small fields with big hedgerows mounted on top of banks. It was difficult for the tank driver, and the enemy tanks, anti-tank guns and Panzerfausts could operate in these small fields and hedges much more easily against a tank than we could against them. So when we first went into the bocage we did have great problems.

Although often quoted in accounts of the Normandy Campaign, this following exchange between two British tankers gives a flavour of how advancing in such country into the face of cleverly camouflaged and screened defensive positions – replete with carefully deployed panzers such as the Panther – took immense courage:

'What do the Germans have most of?'
    'Panthers. Panthers can slice through a Churchill like butter from a mile away.'
    'And how does a Churchill get a Panther?'
    'It creeps up on it. When it reaches close quarters the gunner tries to bounce a shot off the underside of the Panther's gun mantlet. If he's lucky, it goes through a thin piece of armour above the driver's head.'
    'Has anybody ever done it?'
    'Yes, Davis in C Squadron. He's back with headquarters now trying to recover his nerve.'

RIGHT A Panther Ausf G prepares to drive into the terrain so characteristic of the bocage country.

Montgomery, the Allied ground commander, had not expected to have to fight in the bocage for an extended period, as in his original planning Caen was scheduled to have fallen on 6 June. That it did not do so in the face of a strong German defence saw the British Army

having to fight 'a campaign through terrain for which it had little prepared'. He chose to launch a whole succession of limited, but rolling offensives to the west of Caen, and directly through the bocage. Under various names – Operations Perch, Epsom, Windsor, Charnwood and Jupiter – the British and Canadians pushed southward at cost, which nonetheless proved ruinous to the German defenders, as the men and equipment they lost could rarely be made up for by replacements. Although German figures for the period to 3 July claimed that 537 Allied tanks had been destroyed, of which 227 were attributed to the panzers, the Allied losses could be absorbed and replaced. By contrast, of the 349 panzers lost up to 8 July, 112 were Panthers, a figure that had risen to

131 by the 27th of that month. Replacements were received, but simply never in great enough numbers to compensate for the losses.

However, the inherent advantages of the Panther vis-à-vis Allied armour could be negated by the employment of poor tactics by their users. The example cited here is of the 12th SS Panzer Divison. On 12 June, 'Panzer' Meyer had ordered a single Panther company – the 3rd SS Pz.Co, with its 12 Panthers – to attack the village of Norrey, held by Canadian troops.

Michael Reynolds, in his history of I SS Panzer Corps in Normandy, describes the Panthers as attacking in line, 'like an old-fashioned cavalry charge'. They had no supporting infantry, and as he says, 'they were

BELOW A Panther as the Propaganda Kompanie cameraman liked to see it. Standing proud of the close country and looking every inch a beast of prey!

totally unaware that the tanks promised to the Reginas [the previous day] had arrived at 05.15 hours'. These were deployed and under cover. What now occurred was described by SS Sergeant Morawetz, who was in one of the Panthers:

We reached completely flat terrain, meadows and fields. Half ahead of us lay Norrey. The whole company drove as a body, at high speed and without any stops, in a broad front . . . after a muffled bang and a swaying, as if the track had been ripped off, the vehicle came to a stop. It was quiet inside the vehicle. I thought we had driven onto a mine. When I looked to the left . . .
I happened to see the turret being torn off the Panther driving on my left-hand flank. At the same moment after another minor explosion, my vehicle began to burn . . . Paul Veith, the gunner sitting in front of me . . . did not move. . . . I jumped out. . . . Then I saw flames coming out of the open hatch as if from a blowtorch . . . to my left, along the same line as my vehicle, other burning Panzers.

The survivors were under heavy enemy fire from machine guns and artillery, 'some of it from naval artillery'. Seven Panthers were lost out of those that began the charge. Nonetheless, a truism for both sides was that offensive action in the bocage brought casualties. German losses in armour increased when they broke cover, and for the Panther, close-order fighting – which prevented them from maximising the advantage of their main gun – then exposed their vulnerable flanks unless provision had been made beforehand for infantry and other armour – such as the Panzer IV – to provide it. The previous account showed that the Panther was vulnerable to Allied fire when such provision was not made. Another account from the war diary of the British 8th Armoured Brigade for 1 July was entitled 'Lessons Learnt' and involved the standard 75mm MV-armed Shermans:

Four Panthers first appeared motoring eastwards straight across the censor at a distance of about 800–850 yards [730–777m]. . . . One Panther was knocked out immediately

DEALING WITH THE PANTHER – THE ALLIED EXPERIENCE

There is no question that for the British, Canadian and US armies the encounter with the Panther for the first time in large numbers in Normandy was to prove a salutary experience – much as it had done for the Red Army in the summer of the previous year. Such were the perceived losses inflicted by the German tank that it became a matter of political debate in the British House of Commons, where it was imputed that British troops were fighting the Germans with inferior tanks. While from the standpoint of morale Montgomery had to stamp on this sort of talk, there was undoubtedly some truth in the matter but, as with almost all things, it was a little more complex an issue than it first appeared.

British tanks had lagged behind those of the Germans from almost the start of the conflict. This applied to tank design as well as to armament design. In consequence of the dissatisfaction with both, the British Army had by 1944 adopted the US M4 as its primary combat tank, but it also adopted the US 75mm MV gun as its standard armament, even for its own domestically produced tanks, as in the Cromwell and the Churchill. This allowed for continuity with the US in tank armament for the M4, but the gun itself had a low muzzle velocity and was unable to penetrate the Panther at battle ranges – hence the short anecdotal account related above.

and brewed up. . . . The other three made no attempt to deploy . . . nor did they traverse their turrets. They were all knocked out and all of them brewed up nicely.

A Panther then appeared at about 1,050 yards (959m).

It was engaged and hit several times on the front with AP but with no effect. HE was then fired at the front with [the] object of blinding the crew. This was apparently successful, for some members of the crew were seen to bale out. The four other Panthers knocked out during the day were all from 800–1,000 yards (731–914m) distance and were all hit in the flank by our 75mm guns.

Thus eight Panthers were knocked out 'for the loss of three of our tanks'.

It was also the case that the fighting in Normandy showed up the other continuing weaknesses of the Panther. On 28 June, Guderian observed in a report to Hitler that while the Panther had proven itself to be a

good tank, it nonetheless, 'burns astonishingly quickly'. He also noted that the lifespan of the Panther's engine (1,400–1,500km) was considerably higher than the Panther's final drives. 'A solution is urgently needed!'

We have noted elsewhere that after the battle for Normandy was over and Allied assessment teams studied the German wrecks that had been left on the battlefield, at least half of all the Panthers they examined had been abandoned because of failed final drives.

The Cromwell and Churchill tanks represented the continuing British anachronism of classifying tanks as either 'cruiser' or 'infantry'. Both the M4 and the Cromwell were classified as the former and the Churchill as the latter. However, after the British had developed the 17pdr anti-tank gun, it possessed a weapon that under most conditions encountered in Normandy allowed it to defeat the Panther, and sometimes the Tiger. As already related, when mounted on the M4 and rechristened the Firefly it provided the Allies with their most effective tank in Normandy. However, on 6 June there were few in service.

Neither the British nor the Americans had developed a heavy tank on a par with the Tiger and indeed both nations, particularly the Americans, regarded the Panther as a heavy tank, thus assuming, that like the Tiger, it would not be encountered in large numbers. It was this complacency, allied to the tank destroyer doctrine, which posed such problems for the US Army when they realised that the Panther, for all its weight, was used by the Germans as a medium tank. It was official doctrine that it was not the job of the tank to fight other tanks – that was the job of the tank-destroyer arm. At the start of the Normandy Campaign this was served by the M10, a lightly armoured machine armed with a 3in gun. Guidelines stated the role of the tank was to exploit breakthroughs in enemy lines and that as this was expected to be executed with speed, this naturally impacted on the amount of armour equipped by the M4. The frontal glacis of the M4 was relatively thin when compared with the Panther and could be penetrated with ease at distance by its main gun. Speed was not to be sacrificed for armour.

Even before the Normandy landings, a 76mm high-velocity gun had been available for the M4 but this had been rejected, even by the likes of Patton, as being not needed. The rationale for this was that the 75m MV gun carried by the M4 had proven effective up until then, and in any case it was assumed it would be employed more to fire HE on 'soft targets', than AP against armour. It was only once the campaign had begun and tanks fought tanks that the cry went up from US tankers for a tank or at least a gun that could take on the Panther, which was in due course to become a real bogeyman for many M4 crews. But even when the 76mm-armed M4 A1 first saw service with Patton's Third Army it was not as effective as hoped for. That being said, US M4 units quickly developed new tactics to compensate for the perceived limitations of their charges.

Even so, it was apparent a new heavy tank was needed and when, finally, the M26 Pershing arrived in Europe towards the end of 1944, it like the Russian IS-II, still weighed less than the Panther medium tank!

It has been argued, and this is a view that this author would support, that the principal problem for the Allies in in Normandy was the terrain. Neither the British nor the Americans had trained to operate in the bocage as it was assumed prior to the D-Day landings that they would not be fighting such conditions. It was the failure to take Caen on day one that denied the British and Canadian forces the open terrain to the east of the city. They thus found themselves having to fight their way through the bocage country to its east and at a high cost. It was, however, a salutary learning experience and it was inevitable that lightly armoured tanks such as the M4 and Cromwell would be bound to suffer. They were thus required to do a job for which they had not been designed. And although the Panther preferred the wide-open steppe to employ its main gun, its essentially defensive role throughout the campaign permitted it to inflict heavy damage on the Allied tank force. But, as in the East, the Allies by hook and by crook – and by guile – were able to master the beast.

The need to adapt – very different German tactics

It was the facticity of the aforementioned constraints on their operations that dictated German tank tactics in the bocage in

ABOVE A Panther Ausf A has chosen to leave the road and plunge through a hedge – just the sort of action that led to the *Schürzen* being torn away.

Normandy. It was Guderian who spelt out that in Normandy 'the terrain was unsuitable for panzers' – something that all German tankers operating there knew themselves in any case – so that the standard operating technique of employing armour in concentration had to be forgone in favour of organising them into *Panzerjagdkommandos* or so-called *Panzerkampftruppen*. These were small units consisting, given our focus, of just a few Panthers standing 'ready directly behind the front line. Their tasks are immediate counterstrike and destroy enemy tanks that have broken through.'

Panzers were thus disabused of their primary role and were now to be directed by the *Panzergrenadiere* and *Grenadiere.* For the first time in the conflict the panzers were operating in essentially an infantry-support role. Where, however, the Panthers were tasked with maintaining the security of a particular line of defence, they fought enemy forces attacking the first lines of defence – and where they could at the greatest range possible – with local fire control from previously surveyed positions. After a few rounds Panthers would need to change location – the heavy blast of their main gun would require such, as it served to give away their positions – according to plan so as to

avoid a counterstroke by the enemy. A *Panzer Zug* (platoon) could secure a front line of at least 200m – with 50m between each tank. The larger *Panzer Kompanie* was deployed to secure at least a 1,000–1,500m long front line. Where Panthers were attacked from the front, they were virtually invincible by virtue of their heavy frontal armour and the long range of their main gun. It was in situations like this that the British and Canadian tankers suffered their highest losses as they had little choice but to attack frontally, unable to see the camouflaged German panzers hiding amidst the hedgerows until the first M4 or Cromwell 'brewed up'.

The urgency to get more Panther units into combat did not prevent problems occurring in the chaotic conditions along the invasion front which saw at least one fully equipped formation – II/Panzer Regiment 33 of 9th Pz.Div – which had been rebuilt at Mailly-le-Camp with 79 Panthers make little contribution. According to the author Nicklas Zetterling in his book *Normandy 1944:*

This battalion was sent back and forth between various units and it seems to have made little combat contribution. It seems that it was first intended to use the Panther battalion in the Mortain attack, but it did not arrive in time. On 9 August, it was decided to send the battalion to the II SS Pz Corps. Two days later it was on its way to the LVIII. Pz Corps. It was expected that 4 tanks would arrive on the morning of 11 August and a further 20 on the morning of the following day. The other tanks of the battalion were unavailable due to mechanical problems suffered during all the movements. On 14 August the battalion was placed under the operational control of the 116th Pz.Div. Almost surprisingly it remained with that division the following day. The battalion had not been in combat previously: it had about 25 operational vehicles.

Nonetheless, this formation was one of the few Panther-equipped units to survive the eventual destruction of Army Group West in the Falaise Pocket.

The greatest success of the Panther occurred in helping to 'see down' the great British armoured thrust to the east of Caen, in the operation known as Goodwood. Between 18 and 20 July, three British armoured divisions advanced across open and rolling terrain, pocked by villages and with a gentle rise up to the Bourguébus Ridge that had been fortified by

Rommel with five lines of defences supported by mobile reserves of Panzer IV, Panther and Tiger battalions. A huge aerial bombardment designed to eliminate these armoured reserves failed in its execution, such that when the mass of British armour started advancing, large numbers of tanks were knocked out by anti-tank guns sited in the undamaged villages. When the Panthers and the few Tigers advanced forward to the crest of the ridge they began to execute destruction on the advancing British tanks with their long-range gunnery. But they then began to suffer losses as they left the ridgeline and descended the slope to engage the enemy at ranges of 1,000m or less. Panthers were lost to Fireflies. Over the course of the operation the British lost over 400 machines, although not all were total losses. Many were recovered. Although German losses in armour were not high, they still represented a further drain on declining numbers.

On 2 July, the *Panzer Lehr* was shifted to the west opposite the US forces in the south of the Cotentin Peninsula. Its place in the line was taken by II SS Pz.Div. This formation had been substantially whittled down since its arrival in the first week of the invasion. On 1 July it had 32 Panthers combat ready and 26 in repair with

BELOW The Jagdpanther went into action with s.Pz.Jg.Abt 654 in Normandy. Very few survived to escape the closing of the Falaise Pocket, as did this one. Many others were left abandoned with broken final drives.

8 replacement Panthers having been sent on 28 June. Following an abortive attack on 11 July towards the Vire Canal, which cost them at least 30 tanks the bulk of which were Panthers, PL remained in place to the north and north-west of St Lô until 25 July, when the Americans launched Operation Cobra. On that date the formation had just 30 Panthers combat ready and 26 under repair. Further to the west was deployed *Das Reich* which had 21 Panthers combat ready and 29 in short-term repair. The Americans had 477 M4s and 316 M5 light tanks ready for their offensive. Here is not the place to describe this battle in detail, suffice it to say that following a massive bombing operation and artillery barrage the launch of the US ground forces had led, by the end of the day, to the total disruption of the German front and their subsequent retreat. *Das Reich*, with some of its Panthers and the remnants of 17th SS Div, had been encircled around the town of Roncey. Even as the US Army was driving south through and beyond Avranches in the days after the beginning of Cobra, the British launched Operation Bluecoat, the purposes of which was to pin down the westward movement of German armoured formations. It was in this operation that the Jagdpanthers of s.Pz. Jg.Abt 654 saw action for the first time. Three Jagdpanthers destroyed eleven Churchill tanks before withdrawing but abandoning two of their own.

With the US Army plunging southward beyond Avranches, Hitler, on 4 August, was pondering the maps of Normandy hundreds of miles away, had jabbed his finger at this town at the western base of the Cotentin Peninsula, and ordered a counter-attack that would thrust across the US rear and cut them off. This became Operation *Lüttich*. Hitler ordered von Kluge, the German commander, that he employ all eight panzer divisions for the operation. As it was, only about 180 panzers, assault guns and *PanzerJäger* could be released for the operation – a far smaller number than Hitler had demanded. Of these, 70 were Panthers. Unsurprisingly, the Americans were forewarned, by Ultra intercepts, of the operation, which was eventually launched on 7 August and was brought to a halt just over a day later. A column of German armour, caught on the road by

Jabos (German slang for fighter-bombers), was destroyed, this including 46 panzers of which 33 were Panthers. Although Hitler ordered it relaunched, the whole matter was over by 13 August for even as *Lüttich* was under way, Montgomery launched a major offensive called 'Totalize' to the south and east of Caen with the intention of breaking through to Falaise some 16 miles to the south. Launched at night on 7/8 August, it caught the Germans by surprise. By dawn the Canadians, who were leading the assault, were 3 miles into the German lines. Very heavy fighting now took place with the Panthers of the 12th SS Panzer Division *Hitler Jugend* putting up very heavy resistance, in consequence of which, by 11 August, Montgomery had called the operation off. This formation had been in action since a few days after D-Day and had fought extremely hard and garnered for itself an infamous reputation. According to Zetterling, as of 4 August, the Panther battalion had 59 of the panzers on strength with an unknown number in repair.

Although the US thrust southward from Avranches was originally targeting the river Seine, the discovery of very limited German forces offered up the possibility of a left hook into the rear of the German forces in Normandy. The final British offensive of the Normandy Campaign, codenamed Tractable, was launched on 14 August and by the 16th the Canadians had broken through to Falaise. It was now apparent to the Germans that all of their forces in Normandy were in danger of being encircled, so Field Marshal Model, the new field commander, ordered the immediate withdrawal of all German forces through the Argentan–Falaise Gap. As the Germans attempted to do just that, there was extremely heavy fighting as battlegroups equipped with Panthers and other panzers attempted to keep the Allied jaws apart. They succeeded until 21 August when they finally snapped shut.

The measure of the loss of Panthers in this campaign is that by the beginning of September there were only three units that were able to field this panzer: I./Pz.Rgt 24, II./Pz.Rgt 33 and I./Pz.Rgt 15. All the others of the many committed to the Invasion Front between June and the end of August had been destroyed, abandoned or, if they had succeeded in evading the encirclement at Falaise, had been lost subsequently in the retreat to the Seine. That being said, there is little doubt that the Panther, even more than the much-lauded Tiger, was the most significant German tank in the campaign and had inflicted a heavy cost on the Allies for their victory. However, it is also clear that the Panther was far from being a paragon, as General Fritz Bayerlein, the commander of *Panzer Lehr* – and a highly experienced panzer commander – opined. He had after all commanded not only the most powerful panzer division in the German Army on 6 June, but it also had the most powerful Panther formation, with 88 on strength. His opinion is worthy of study:

> *While the Pz.Kpfw IV could be used to advantage, the Pz.Kpfw V – the Panther – proved ill adapted to the terrain. The Sherman because of its manoeuvrability and height was good. The Panther was poorly suited for hedgerow terrain because of its width, long barrel, and width of tank reduced its manoeuvrability in village and forest fighting. It is very front-heavy and therefore quickly wears out the final drives, made of low-grade steel. High silhouette. Very sensitive power train requiring well-trained drivers. Weak side armour; tank top vulnerable to fighter bombers. Fuel lines of porous material that allows gas fumes to escape into the tank interior causing a grave fire hazard. Absence of vision slits makes defence against close attack impossible.*

But he also acknowledged its strengths: 'An ideal vehicle for tank battles and infantry support. The best tank in existence for its weight.'

BELOW The lot of German armour abandoned in Normandy. Collected together and awaiting the scrappers' torches. At least two Panthers can be seen amidst this detritus of war.

The status of the Panther on the Eastern and Western Fronts after August 1944

With the end of the fighting in Normandy and the temporary hiatus on the Eastern Front, it was clear that the German Army had suffered a number of catastrophic defeats. From our perspective, with our focus on the Panther tank, it can be said that wherever the *Panzerwaffe* was operative, so too were Panther units. But losses in this tank – as with the other types seeing service at this time – had been grievous.

On the eve of the launch of Operation Bagration by the Red Army on 22 June 1944, strength returns had indicated that the *Panzerwaffe* in the East could field 1,200 heavy and medium tanks, of which 313 were Panthers. In the preceding six months, 752 of the total of 2,505 panzers lost had been Panthers, with the majority being in Russia and a much smaller number in Italy. From June onwards, numbers of lost tanks increased markedly, such that between July and September strength returns indicated that of the total of 2,625 tanks 'lost', just under a thousand – specifically 923 Panthers – had been written off. The Panthers leaving the factories in (a) July and August and (b) in August and September, were employed to replace another 513 lost in period (a) and 764 Panthers in period (b). The breakdown of allocation of replacements was as follows:

Eastern Front No lost/no of replacements	Western Front No lost/no of replacements	Italian Front No lost/no of replacements
(a) July/August	(a) July/August	(a) July/August
258/236	207/370	48/38
(b) August/September	(b) August/September	(b) August/September
132/186	543/284	22/20

The decline in the number of replacements in August and September reflects the allocation of the difference in the amount produced to equip several new formations. These were the new Panzer Brigades – smaller than a division – of which 14 were created at the behest of Hitler, who was of the view that these more compact formations could be deployed more rapidly to counter enemy breakthroughs. Ostensibly created for service on the Eastern Front, they first saw widespread use on the Western Front when seven of these formations were deployed to face down the Allied drive on Germany's borders where they clashed with the advancing US Army forces. The speed with which they had been established did not augur well for their success in combat as is confirmed by a report of the fate of the Pz.Brig 112. It is telling, inasmuch as its deployment suggests little experience of combat as one of the realities facing the Army at the time was a severe shortage in manpower and the great loss of experienced tank crews. The brigade was sent into action on 12/13 September against:

. . . the American breakthrough southwest of Epinal. During this necessary action, the Brigade lost almost all of its Panthers [author's emphasis] and half of its Panzer IVs to fighter-bomber attacks, artillery fire and tanks. The I. (Panther) Abteilung/Panzer regiment 29 was practically destroyed. They still possess four operational Panthers. A further three Panthers and a Befehlspanther are in need of repair. Thirty-four Panthers are a total write-off. During this action, practically no mechanical breakdowns occurred.

The description also provides graphic evidence that the US Army had come a long way since the invasion in June in terms of being able to deal with the Panther. This is also reflected in another German account. Some days later a Leutnant Schreiber in the very first action of Pz.Abt 218 with Pz.Brig 108:

The assembly area was on a height in plain view of the opponent and probably was also observed. The attack was launched without artillery preparation. The Panthers attacked over a small ridge into the opponent's

position. *The Panthers received well-aimed anti-tank fire from a range of 10–20m. The Panthers were total write-offs, and several others required extensive repairs . . . the Panzer-Grenadiere that were following the Panthers in their SPWs had heavy losses in SPWs and personnel.*

The notion of the Panzer Brigade was subsequently deemed to have been a dismal failure, and they were rapidly disbanded with their assets reallocated to the standard Pz.Rgts. In light of the Führer's revelation that, come the winter, he intended to launch a counter-offensive through the Ardennes forest region

ABOVE A late-model Panther Ausf G equipped with the chine at the base of the mantlet being inspected by a US Army officer. It also possesses the heating tower on the rear deck that places this as a late-production machine.

LEFT Another late Panther Ausf G, built after October 1944, is seen here abandoned on 26 December 1944 during the Battle of the Bulge.

so as to reach Antwerp – thereby splitting the western Allies – a determined attempt was made to accumulate the necessary resources to conduct it. From October onward, there was a deliberate policy of holding back on the delivery of replacement panzers so as to build up the necessary forces for what came to be called, by the Germans, Operations *Wacht am Rhein* and *Nordwind.* That being said, at least three units – namely I./Pz.Rgt 6, I./Pz.Rgt 11 and I./Pz.Rgt 130 – were sent to the Eastern Front, with each fielding 60 new Panthers.

Thomas Jentz has shown that over the period of what has come to be called 'The Battle of the Bulge', on 'the other side of the hill' – that is between 15 December 1944 and 15 January 1945 – by which date the operation had been terminated, there were just under 500 Panthers registered as available for the operations. On 15 December there were 471 (of which 336 were operational), a fortnight later on 30 December 451 were available (of which 240 were operational) and finally on 15 January 487 were available (of which just 221 were operational). The differential equated to the number of Panthers either lost or in need of repair.

The end

During the period of October–November 1944 there were some 684 Panthers serving on the Eastern Front deployed on a front ranging from Courland, northern Poland, and down through to Hungary, while in the West there were 371 and in Italy just 39. These figures should be set against a total inventory registered as being 1,729, with 1,094 of that number actually in service. Losses of Panthers in December 1944 on all fronts totalled 234. Included in this figure were those already lost in the Ardennes operation up until the end of that month, with these making a grand total of 2,680 Panthers lost in the whole of 1944. A mere 110 of this number were recovered, repaired and returned to service. That this number was so low was on account of the retreat of the German Army on all fronts, being such that even moderately damaged Panthers could not be retrieved, and thus fell into the hands of the Red Army and the Western Allies.

When the massive Soviet offensive into Poland began in January 1945, those Panthers serving in Courland were totally isolated and thus denied to the German panzer forces attempting to defend against massive Red

Army assaults that ultimately carried it through to the river Oder by April 1945. The attempted defence of Poland and southward through to Hungary also saw the Soviets drive westward and into Austria. The very last offensive operation launched by the Germans occurred between 1 and 26 January 1945, when IV SS Pz.Corps attempted to relieve those forces trapped in Budapest. Initial and limited gains were made, but by the end of the month the operation had petered out. Panthers were ubiquitous in all panzer operations in the East and they were still able to inflict local victories over the advancing Soviet forces. However, the reality was that defeat for Germany was now inevitable. The forces facing Germany on both fronts proved overwhelming. The Panther's final hurrah was in the combating of the Red Army's crossing of the river Oder on the Seelow Heights.

In the same fashion, Panthers were encountered by the British, Canadian and US Forces through to the German surrender in May.

Before that, and symptomatic of the growing chaos and reality of approaching defeat (even if admittance of this was anathema to Hitler), was a final attempt, made in January 1945, to bring some semblance of rational order to tank output with an emergency Panzer Production Programme. It was the critical shortage of vital raw materials and the growing damage to tank production facilities, as they were relentlessly targeted by Allied bombing raids, which prompted this. This was reflected in the monthly production figures which saw just 285 Panthers produced in December 1944.

Although MAN had accrued a considerable stock of some parts for Panther production – enough, it is said, for at least 400 panzers – it was the inability and failure of strategic suppliers to provide, for example, items such as the hull and turret housing, that brought the curtain down on Panther production in the plan, and it was ordered that both it and the Tiger II would cease production at the end of May 1945. Until then, targets for Panther production were set

BELOW A late Panther Ausf G wearing a similar camouflage scheme as that seen on the Bovington Panther in Chapter 4. The picture was taken on the Oder Front before the launch of the final Soviet offensive to take Berlin.

down as follows: 275 were to be produced in February and 290 in March and April with the termination of production thereafter. As it was, even amidst the chaos and the growing Allied advance into Germany itself, there was a last flourish of Panther production as MAN, DB and MNH produced 439 by the time hostilities ceased. This meant that as of 15 March, there were still 954 Panthers on strength with the field army, with 446 of these in service in the East and 152 on the Western Front, plus a token 24 in Italy. As the fighting continued right up to the surrender, these numbers had reduced by the time that occurred.

A short Panther footnote – post-war service in the French Army

Although the Panther's career in the Heer was over with the end of the war in Europe, a small number would finish up being used by one of Nazi Germany's former enemies. Indeed, its period of service with the French Army would exceed its employment by that of the German.

The very many Panthers abandoned in France in the wake of the Wehrmacht's retreat in 1944 and the number salvaged by the French occupation forces in Germany following its surrender permitted the French Army to contemplate the use of the Panther as part of its rebuilding process in the months and years after the conflict.

In 1947, a regiment of Panthers – namely the 503rd Armoured Regiment – was established in the Camp de Mourmelon in the Marne départment. Fifty Panthers had been overhauled and then issued to this regiment. Other Panthers and a few Jagdpanthers were also stationed at the French Army's tank training ground at Mailly-le-Camp and at Satory. These stayed in service until 1950 when they were replaced. It was in 1947 that the French Army produced a very objective report on the machine, entitled *Le Panther 1947*, and which has been cited quite extensively in this short work.

There had been some discussion whether to send Panthers to Indo-China as part of the French forces tasked with reclaiming the region for the republic. However, the recognition that the Panther was 'not a strategic tank' put paid to that notion. Thus, it was in the French Army that the Panther saw its final service.

Reflections

The degree of fascination that German tanks of the Second World War continues to exert on the public is remarkable, with that interest being primarily directed at the Tiger I heavy tank and also, at the subject of this work, the Panther medium tank. Indeed, it would seem to go further than just fascination, as many individuals seem to endow these machines with an almost mystic and mythic quality. From the perspective of the author, the Panther is a fascinating machine, but (and it is a big but), it was not a paragon. It had many flaws, some of which were never cured and impacted upon the machine's performance from the first day it entered combat to the last. Therefore, any objective account of the Panther must depict it 'warts and all'.

It was created remarkably quickly, and that is a testament to its designers, but they had to work with what was available. As we have seen, the engine, transmission and final drive were all flawed in their own ways – had they performed as hoped, then the Panther would truly have been a most formidable fighting machine. But they did not. Thus German tankers were equipped with a most intimidatingly armed and frontally armoured tank but they had nonetheless to be very careful, if not delicate with the engine, gearbox and final drive. Too many Panthers were unserviceable because of problems with the road wheels and the failure of those other essential elements. And it has to be said, a Panther that was unserviceable was equal to a Panther that was lost, irrespective of how good the specification of this machine was on paper. It was these limitations that precluded the Panther being considered by the French Army (which actually operated their Panthers for longer than did the German Army after the war) as a 'strategic tank'. Meaning that it could not have embarked on the wide-ranging offensive operations that characterised the operations of the much lighter Panzers III and IV in the first three years of the conflict. Nor could it have emulated the speed and rapid advance of the M4s and Cromwell tanks of the Allies in the period after the breakout from Normandy.

While by 1944 the Panther was certainly a more effective fighting machine than when it first went into combat at Kursk in July of the previous year, the total losses incurred on the three fronts on which it fought in 1944 were nonetheless very high. While acknowledging that it was a most formidable opponent, it could nonetheless be defeated and the longer the Soviet, US and Commonwealth troops fought against it, the more they were able to develop effective tactics to cope with it. That being said, no tanker, be they Soviet, American or Commonwealth, would deny that the Panther remained a most formidable opponent to the very end of the war in Europe and one that had to be dealt with very carefully indeed. However, following the huge German defeat in the East in the summer of 1944 and the Allied breakout from Normandy, as much as German tank losses were high, so too were those of experienced German tank crew – whether they had been killed or captured. Indeed, it could be argued that the performance of the Panther after these huge defeats was not as effective simply because tank crews that had learnt to deal with the idiosyncrasies of the machine through the experience of operating it, were no longer to hand in significant numbers. In the closing months of the war, training was short and younger Panther drivers had none of that to draw upon.

Is it heretical to ask the question: was the Panther the tank the German Army really needed in the latter half of the war? Were the core assumptions that underpinned the design at its outset, the correct ones, namely that quality must trump quantity as being the only way in which the German Army could hope to neutralise superior Russian and Allied numbers. And, secondly, the assumption that heavier armour must ensure the longer survival of the Panther in combat. Even Guderian had given voice to his doubt about the latter in his report of the Panzers in Normandy when he had opined that 'our tanks are too heavy', this being a reference to the Panther, Tiger I and Tiger II.

A possible answer to these questions can perhaps be offered by Albert Speer, the German Munitions Minister, when on a fact-finding tour in northern Italy between 19 and 25 October 1944. The conclusions are interesting – and it has to be said they would not have been shared by all German tankers. They also lend a different German perspective on the American M4. Speer noted:

On the Southwest Front, opinions are in favour of the Sherman tank and its cross-country ability. The Sherman tank climbs mountains that our Panzer crews consider impassable. This is accomplished by the especially powerful engine in the Sherman in comparison to its weight. Also, according to the reports of the 26.Panzer Division [which had a Panther regiment] the terrain-crossing ability on level ground [in the Po valley] is completely superior to our Panzers. The Sherman tanks drive freely cross-country, while our Panzers must remain on trails and narrow roads and therefore are very restricted in their ability to fight. All Panzer crews want to receive lighter Panzers [and although he does not say so, this must be a reference to lighter than the Panther], which are more manoeuvrable, possess increased ability to cross terrain, and guarantee the necessary combat power just with a superior gun.

Ten years after the end of the Second World War in Europe, West Germany began the process of creating a new army. Although initially equipped with US tanks, in 1957 the Bundeswehr issued its specification for a new German tank. Interestingly, it drew on almost next to nothing from the Panther design, other than being named for yet another member of the cat family (albeit gaining the name Leopard only in 1963). Its weight at 30 tons, was 15 less than that of the Panther G. It was to have a power-to-weight ratio of 30hp, a road speed of 65km/h, and an off-road speed of 40km/h. It was to be armed with a British-derived 105mm main gun, with a penetration capability of 150mm of RHA at a combat range of up to 2,500m. Speed was to compensate for thinner armour and it was to be powered by a diesel engine. Armed with the 75mm L/70, this may well have been the tank the Germans needed in 1943!

The legacy of the Panther lay more in the manner in which it influenced the design of foreign tanks. The British Centurion, without doubt one of the most successful tank designs since 1945, aped its shape and the thickness of its armour. However, it eschewed the overlapping road wheel suspension – a feature not soon on any post-war tank. Like the Panther, it had a powerful main gun, its last battle tank variant fielding the same 105mm as the new Leopard.

Panther Ausf G specifications

Crew: 5

Weight, combat loaded: 99,873lb

Performance
Max speed, road: 28.39mph (45.7km/h)
Max speed, cross-country: 15.5–18.6mph
(25–30km/h)
Max gradient: 30 degrees
Fording depth: 6ft 3in
Trench crossing: 8ft 0in
Range (internal fuel): 124 miles (200km)
Cross-country: 62 miles (100km)

Dimensions
Length overall: 29ft ¾in (886cm)
Length: 22ft 9in (693.5cm)
Width overall: 10ft 8¾in (327cm)
Height: 9ft 10in (299.5cm)
Ground clearance: 1ft 10in (56cm)
Fire height of gun: 7ft 7in (230cm)
Turret ring diameter: 5ft 5in (165cm)
Road wheel diameter: 2ft 9in (86cm)
Road wheel width: 4in (10cm)

Engine
1 Maybach HL 230P30 V-12 (60 degrees) OHV
water-cooled petrol of 23.88 litres developing
700bhp at 3,000rpm. 12V electrical system

Steering
MAN multi-geared

Armament
Main: 1 × 75mm KwK43 L/70
Traverse: 360 degrees
Elevation: +20 degrees, –4 degrees
Secondary armament: 2 × 7.92 MG 34 (plus
option for ring-mount)
1 × *Nahverteidigungswaffe*

Stowage
Ammunition: 75mm – 82 rounds
Ammunition: 7.92mm – 4,800 rounds

Armour
Nose upper (glacis): 80mm @ 35 degrees
Nose lower: 80mm @ 55 degrees
Sides – upper: 40mm @ 60 degrees
Sides – lower: 40mm @ 90 degrees
Rear: 40mm @ 60 degrees
Decking: 15mm @ 0 degrees
Belly – front: 20mm @ 0 degrees
Belly – rear: 13mm @ 0 degrees
Turret front: 100mm @ 80 degrees
Turret sides: 45 mm @ 65 degrees
Turret rear: 45mm @ 62 degrees
Turret roof: 15mm @ 0 and 6 degrees
Mantlet: 120mm rounded

Vision
Driver: 1 rotating periscope
Radio operator: 1 periscope and MG sight
Commander: 7 periscopes
Gun loader: 1 periscope.

Select bibliography

Anderson, Thomas, *Panther* (Osprey, 2017)

Anderson, Thomas, *The History of the Panzerwaffe*, Vol. 2 (Osprey, 2017)

Bacyk, Norbert, *The Tank Battle at Praga* (Leondoer & Ekholm, 2006)

Buckley, John, *British Armour in Normandy* (Cass, 2004)

Buckley, John ed., *The Normandy Campaign 1944* (Routledge, 2006)

Friedli, Lukas, *Repairing the Panzers*, Vol. 2 (Panzerwrecks, 2011)

Glantz, David and House, Jonathan, *When Titans Clashed* (Kansas, 1995)

Hayward, Mark, *Sherman Firefly* (Barbarossa Books, 2001)

Healy, Mark, *Zitadelle* (The History Press, 2008)

Healy, Mark, *T-34 Tank* (Haynes, 2018)

Isby, David, *Fighting in Normandy* (Greenhill Books, 2001)

Jentz, Thomas, *Germany's Panther Tank* (Schiffer Publishing, 1995)

Jentz, Thomas, *Panzer Truppen*, Vol. 2 (Schiffer Publishing, 1997)

Jung, Hans-Joachim, *Panzer Regiment Grossdeutschland* (Fedorowicz, 2000)

Lefevre, Eric, *Panzers in Normandy: Then and Now* (After the Battle, 1983)

MacDougall, Roddy and Block, Martin, *Panther: External Appearance and Design Changes* (Abteilung 532, 2016)

MacDougall, Roddy and Neely, Darren, *Nürnberg's Panzer Factory* (Panzerwrecks, 2013)

Mawdsley, Evan, *Thunder in the East* (Hodder Arnold, 2005)

Mitcham, Samuel, *Panzers in Normandy* (Stackpole Books, 2009)

Ogorkiewicz, Richard, *Tanks – 100 Years of Evolution* (Osprey, 2015)

Quarrie, Bruce, *Encyclopedia of the Germany Army in the 20th Century* (PSL, 1989)

Reynolds, Michael, *Steel Inferno* (Spellmount, 1997)

Seaton, Albert, *The Fall of Fortress Europe 1943–1945* (Batsford, 1981)

Spielberger, Walter, *Panther and its Variants* (Schiffer Publishing, 1993)

Szamveber, Norbert, *Waffen SS Armour in Normandy* (Helion, 2012)

Zetterling, Nicklas, *Normandy 1944* (Fedorowicz, 2000)

The author also wishes to acknowledge the use of the extensive archival material at the Tank Museum, Bovington, Dorset, UK.

Index